Elements in the Philosophy of Immanuel Kant
edited by
Desmond Hogan
*Princeton University*
Howard Williams
*University of Cardiff*
Allen Wood
*Indiana University*

# KANT ON SELF-CONTROL

Marijana Vujošević
*Leiden University and University of Groningen*

Shaftesbury Road, Cambridge CB2 8EA, United Kingdom

One Liberty Plaza, 20th Floor, New York, NY 10006, USA

477 Williamstown Road, Port Melbourne, VIC 3207, Australia

314–321, 3rd Floor, Plot 3, Splendor Forum, Jasola District Centre, New Delhi – 110025, India

103 Penang Road, #05–06/07, Visioncrest Commercial, Singapore 238467

Cambridge University Press is part of Cambridge University Press & Assessment, a department of the University of Cambridge.

We share the University's mission to contribute to society through the pursuit of education, learning and research at the highest international levels of excellence.

www.cambridge.org
Information on this title: www.cambridge.org/9781009486767

DOI: 10.1017/9781108885232

© Marijana Vujošević 2024

This publication is in copyright. Subject to statutory exception and to the provisions of relevant collective licensing agreements, no reproduction of any part may take place without the written permission of Cambridge University Press & Assessment.

When citing this work, please include a reference to the DOI 10.1017/9781108885232

First published 2024

A catalogue record for this publication is available from the British Library.

ISBN 978-1-009-48676-7 Hardback
ISBN 978-1-108-81376-1 Paperback
ISSN 2397-9461 (online)
ISSN 2514-3824 (print)

Cambridge University Press & Assessment has no responsibility for the persistence or accuracy of URLs for external or third-party internet websites referred to in this publication and does not guarantee that any content on such websites is, or will remain, accurate or appropriate.

# Kant on Self-Control

Elements in the Philosophy of Immanuel Kant

DOI: 10.1017/9781108885232
First published online: May 2024

Marijana Vujošević
*Leiden University and University of Groningen*

**Author for correspondence:** Marijana Vujošević,
m.vujosevic@phil.leidenuniv.nl

**Abstract:** This Element considers Kant's conception of self-control and the role it plays in his moral philosophy. It offers a detailed interpretation of the different terms used by Kant to explain the phenomenon of moral self-control, such as 'autocracy' and 'inner freedom'. Following Kant's own suggestions, the proposed reading examines the Kantian capacity for self-control as an ability to 'abstract from' various sensible impressions by looking beyond their influence on the mind. This analysis shows that Kant's conception of moral self-control involves two intimately related levels, which need not meet the same criteria. One level is associated with realizing various ends, the other with setting moral ends. The proposed view most effectively accommodates self-control's role in the adoption of virtuous maxims and ethical end-setting. It explains why self-control is central to Kant's conception of virtue and sheds new light on his discussions of moral strength and moral weakness.

**Keywords:** self-control, autocracy, abstraction, inner freedom, virtue, moral strength and weakness

© Marijana Vujošević 2024

ISBNs: 9781009486767 (HB), 9781108813761 (PB), 9781108885232 (OC)
ISSNs: 2397-9461 (online), 2514-3824 (print)

# Contents

| | | |
|---|---|---|
| 1 | Introduction | 1 |
| 2 | Self-Control through the Lens of 'Autocracy' | 12 |
| 3 | Self-Control as Abstraction and Inner Freedom | 20 |
| 4 | A Twofold Account of Moral Strength | 35 |
| 5 | Moral Weakness: The Other Side of the Coin | 46 |
| 6 | Concluding Remarks | 57 |
| | References | 60 |

# 1 Introduction

## 1.1 Conceptual Contours

Many children like marshmallows. In Walter Mischel's classic studies on delayed gratification, children were asked to resist the temptation to eat a marshmallow when the researcher left the room; they were told that those who resisted this temptation would receive two marshmallows instead of one.[1] Self-control was crucial to realizing the goal of receiving two attractive treats. What is important for our purposes is that this study acknowledges the importance of prudential self-control, which presupposes more-or-less given goals.

Contemporary moral psychology has rightly acknowledged this instrumental kind of self-control, but this has led to the downplaying of another significant form of self-control: resisting the temptation to lower one's moral standards when setting oneself goals.[2] However, although ruthless dictators can be very self-controlled in pursuing their evil goals, the self-control they lack has to do with the temptation to settle for lower standards when adopting their goals. This example suggests that self-control also plays a crucial role in ethical goal-setting. This role may be highlighted by fully clarifying self-control as the ability to redirect attention. Numerous empirical studies confirm the close tie between self-control and attention. To my knowledge, no attempts to explain the relationship between the activity of end-setting and self-control, conceived of as redirected attention, can be found in the available literature on contemporary moral psychology.[3]

In this Element, I address Kant's conception of moral self-control by interpreting it in terms of *abstraction*, understood as the activity of refocusing attention. This interpretation finds support in textual sources. It covers prudential and instrumental self-control but primarily aims to provide a fuller account of the self-control characteristic of Kantian virtue. Instrumental and prudential self-control do not exhaust Kant's notion of moral self-control. Kantian moral self-control should not be downgraded to a mere instrument for compelling ourselves to act on the basis of already adopted principles and ends. It is required not only for realizing predefined ends but also for setting ourselves moral ends. I will try to show that self-control, as a psychological condition, can be central to Kant's conception of virtue – essentially conceived of as free

---

[1] See Mischel (2014).

[2] Even influential accounts that aim to capture self-control's normative aspect, such as those offered by Jeannette Kennett (2003) and Edmund Henden (2008), do not detail the role played by self-control in setting ends.

[3] Sebastian Watzl (2022) explains self-control in terms of attention but only acknowledges its role in realizing ends.

2    *The Philosophy of Immanuel Kant*

self-constraint in end-setting. In order to do so, I will first try to situate Kant's notion of self-control in his moral theory.

One commonly found, and to a considerable extent tenable picture of the relationship between Kant's moral theory and his moral psychology, can be sketched as follows.[4] Try to imagine a moral theory according to which most of our psychological conditions, such as our instincts, natural feelings and desires, are obstacles we must overcome if we are to become virtuous. In this theory, moral agency is broadly conceived as a constant struggle with these psychological obstacles: acting morally requires that we prevent these subjective conditions from influencing our way of thinking. The underlying thought is that practical reason, when determining what is morally right or wrong, should be free from all sensible and personal influences. Only some psychological conditions, such as our cultivated sympathetic feelings, moral feelings, self-control and conscience, may be considered aids to morality, but even these subjective conditions are mere tools that help us to perform moral actions. Such conditions become useful only once we have discerned right from wrong and adopted moral principles – they can be means to observing maxims, but not their necessary conditions.

Self-control rightly plays a crucial role in this picture. Kantian moral agency is often conceived as a struggle with instincts, feelings and inclinations, and dealing with these psychological obstacles requires self-control. The capacity for controlling sensibility (CPrR 5: 159), or the capacity for mastering inclinations (MM 6: 383), is central to Kant's account of virtue. He has been reported as saying that virtue means 'strength in controlling oneself [*Stärke in der Selbstbeherrschung*]' (L-Eth 27: 300). When explaining what virtue as moral strength involves, Kant writes that we must assume that all of us have 'the capacity (*facultas*) to overcome all sensible impulses', suggesting that this capacity is to be called strength if we think of it not as simply given but as acquired by us (MM 6: 397). As I will elaborate, he deems this capacity necessary for acquiring inner freedom, which is the constitutive basis of virtue (MM 6: 408). In the above described case, however, self-control as a psychological condition can only be relevant as a tool for performing morally correct actions.

Attention is usually paid to the context in which Kant mentions self-control (*Selbstbeherrschung*) at the beginning of the *Groundwork of the Metaphysics of Morals* (4: 394), where he argues that qualities such as self-control and the moderation of affects and passions can have only instrumental value. At first glance, Kant's example of the cruel Roman dictator Sulla perfectly illustrates

---

[4] My discussions here draw on Vujošević (2017).

this view: Sulla can be said to have self-control because he steadfastly follows his bad maxims (Anth 7: 293). Although his ends and maxims are not morally acceptable, he is good at compelling himself to perform actions by which he realizes his evil goals and follows his evil maxims. When interpreted merely along these lines, the Kantian capacity for self-control is a tool without which we would be unable to compel ourselves to act as we think we should, whether for moral or other reasons. To the extent that we merely acknowledge self-control's role in following already adopted maxims, we fail to capture the distinctive aspect of moral self-control identified by Kant – its role in the adoption of virtuous maxims and ethical end-setting fails to receive the attention it deserves. As a consequence, virtue as moral strength (as a proper exercise of self-control) and moral weakness (as a lack of such self-control) are also likely to be understood as expressed merely at the level of observing already adopted maxims.[5]

Self-control is a psychological condition (L-Eth 27: 360) that plays a crucial role in Kant's ethics, but this is not to say that self-control is the only subjective condition of Kantian virtue. Kant does not list it together with the four subjective conditions of our moral receptivity – probably because self-control is meant to have a more 'active' status than moral feeling, conscience, love of human beings and self-respect (MM 6: 399–402). It is due to these four psychological conditions that we 'can be put under obligation' (MM 6: 399), and it is through self-control that we put ourselves under obligation.[6]

Despite the abundant textual evidence for and important clarificatory advantages of appealing to the notion of abstraction to explain self-control, Kantian self-control has rarely been viewed through this lens. A thorough analysis of the terms Kant uses to explain the phenomenon of moral self-control, such as 'control (*Beherrschung*)', 'rule (*Herrschaft*)', 'autocracy', 'government (*Regierung*)', 'self-composure', 'inner freedom', 'apathy' and 'free self-constraint', along with his notions of abstraction, cultivation, affect and passion, shows why we should not commit ourselves to the reductive model of self-control suggested by the *Groundwork* passage. This analysis also shows that Kant provides a novel account of moral self-control by offering an alternative not only to the Aristotelian views of continence and the moderation of affects

---

[5] As will be explained, Kantian moral weakness is indeed sometimes understood as a mere failure to act in accordance with our otherwise morally correct maxims.

[6] Unlike the other three conditions of moral receptivity, conscience involves a reflective ability to trigger certain feelings. I have argued that the self-reflective activity of conscience is necessary for screening the incentives on which we base our maxims (Vujošević, 2014). Now I aim to show that self-control facilitates the adoption of virtuous maxims in a different way and that it can even be directly involved in their adoption. By exercising our capacity for self-control, we not only realize various ends but also set ourselves ends, which our virtuous maxims involve.

4        *The Philosophy of Immanuel Kant*

and passions, but also to the Humean model of self-control, conceived as a battle between different types of passions. Even more, if Kantian self-control is more than a mere instrument in the performance of morally good actions, and if we, in this light, rethink its relation to some other important psychological conditions, then we have good reason to buttress the relevance of Kant's moral psychology.

## 1.2 Further Details

The prevalence of the above picture, to which a purely instrumental reading of self-control is tailored, is not without reason. Kant gives us grounds for subscribing to this reconstruction. I first explain why this picture is justified by sketching the contrast between some basic ideas in Kant's moral theory, which hinge on the necessary purity of reason and empirical psychology. I then situate Kant's doctrine of virtue within this pure–impure divide and outline the relevance of certain psychological conditions in this doctrine.

### 1.2.1 A Brief Justification

One of Kant's most influential ideas regarding morality, on which the above picture rests, is present in his *Groundwork* (1785). He claims that the supreme principle of morality can only be his famous 'categorical imperative', for it does not have anything else as its condition. The validity of this principle is not even dependent on a specific kind of moral feeling (G 4: 460). It is only by disregarding all feelings, needs and inclinations that we can evade the heteronomy characteristic of traditional moral theories.

Kant argues that the metaphysics of morals should be 'completely cleansed of everything that may be only empirical' (G 4: 389). It should examine 'the idea of principles of a possible pure will and not the actions or conditions of human volition generally, which for the most part are drawn from psychology' (G 4: 390–91). On a charitable interpretation of these passages, Kant's point is that a metaphysics of morals should be cleansed of everything that is merely empirical, because it is not primarily concerned with our psychological conditions. But even if we accept this interpretation, we must admit that Kant is here downgrading feelings and inclinations in favour of pure reason. He does not waver from this position in later writings. In his *Critique of Practical Reason* (1788), Kant points out that inclinations are 'always burdensome' to us (5: 118) and argues that we must release ourselves from all inclinations when making moral decisions (5: 161).

The idea that reason must be 'pure' seems crucial to explaining not only how we come to know our duties but also how we become morally motivated. Kant's well-known view is that the mere performance of a morally good action is not all that is morally required of us. If I adopt the maxim of helping others because I want to improve my reputation, then I am actually moved to help by my inclination to honour, and my action does not have moral worth. If I am to become morally motivated to perform an action, I must somehow set aside 'impure' sources of motivation so that they do not become my primary motives for action. This point can be further clarified by Kant's late account of how we incorporate incentives into our maxims. We incorporate the incentive of the moral law and the incentives of inclinations (Rel 6: 36), but if we are to be morally motivated we must subordinate the incentives of inclinations to the incentive of the moral law.[7]

With all that said, Kant did discuss psychological issues throughout his writings. Most such discussions occur in his lectures on metaphysics, but they can also be found in the *Critique of Pure Reason* and *Anthropology from a Pragmatic Point of View*. Kant addresses empirical and rational psychology: Since both have the soul as their object, even rational psychology must be partly grounded in an empirical principle (CPR A 342–3/B 400–1; L-Met 28: 263). Psychology 'is the cognition of the object of our inner sense' (L-Met 28: 583). Inner sense is consciousness of what we 'undergo' in time (Anth 7: 161). It is consciousness of the manifold sensible impressions that impose themselves on our minds in different situations. Psychology then involves cognition of ourselves, or our souls, on the basis of the sensible impressions that we receive in time. As such, psychology does not seem to be relevant to the above-outlined moral theory. The empirical content that we receive though inner sense is precisely what Kant advises us to 'cleanse' from the metaphysics of morals. Psychology concerns sensible impressions, whereas the very foundation of Kant's moral theory requires that we disregard all sensible impressions.

### 1.2.2 The Doctrine of Virtue and Our Psychological Conditions

This outline prompts the question of where to place Kant's doctrine of virtue in this pure–impure division. For Kant, 'pure morality' contains 'merely the necessary moral laws of a free will in general', whereas the doctrine of virtue 'considers these laws under the hindrances of the feelings, inclinations, and passions to which human beings are more or less subjected' (CPR A 54–5/B 78–

---

[7] By properly ordering our incentives, or 'the matter' of our maxim, we give our maxim the form on the basis of which it can be judged as morally good (Rel 6: 36). The priority of the form of our maxims is given greater emphasis in Kant's discussions of the thought experiment we can perform to check whether our maxims would qualify as a universal law. The universalization test has been widely discussed in the secondary literature. See, for example, Allen Wood (1999) and Pauline Kleingeld (2017).

6 *The Philosophy of Immanuel Kant*

9). Likewise: pure logic draws nothing from psychology, whereas applied logic makes use of the laws of pure logic '*in concreto*, namely, under the contingent conditions of the subject' (CPR A 54/B 78). Since the doctrine of virtue deals with the problem of how to apply moral laws in real-life situations, it must also be about our empirical, subjective conditions. But to say that a doctrine of virtue must draw on psychology is not to say that it should not be built upon pure grounds. Kant points out that we have a duty to go back to metaphysical principles even in the doctrine of virtue (MM 6: 377). The formal principle of duty must be derived from pure reason.

And yet, on its own, this formal principle does not suffice for a doctrine of virtue. Were this the case, this doctrine would simply be a doctrine of morals. What a doctrine of virtue adds to the categorical imperative is that 'this principle is to be thought as the law of your own will and not of will in general' (MM 6: 389). We endorse the categorical imperative by adopting the maxims in accordance with which it demands that we act. The basic principle of the doctrine of virtue is therefore: 'act in accordance with a maxim of ends [*Maxime der Zwecke*] that it can be a universal law for everyone to have' (MM 6: 395). Maxims of ends, or maxims of virtue (*Tugendmaximen*), are particular self-imposed principles on which we really act. As Kant explains, 'a maxim of virtue ... implies that the law itself ... must serve as our incentive' (MM 6: 480). If we are to become morally motivated to perform an action, we must adopt a maxim of virtue by which the moral law becomes the incentive that is powerful enough to move us to perform that action. Mere awareness of the moral law does not suffice. We should also make the moral law an incentive that is by itself sufficient to actually determine our choice. A doctrine of virtue cannot only be about the formal principle of duty – it must also explain how we adopt maxims of virtue. Hence, we also need to determine whether certain psychological conditions are required for the adoption of maxims of virtue.

Over the past few decades, the subjective conditions that make human morality possible, such as self-control, conscience and moral feeling, have been addressed in greater detail.[8] Feelings and inclinations, as subjective human conditions that mostly hinder virtuous action, have also been discussed at length – especially affects and passions.[9] Against the common caricature of the Kantian virtuous agent as someone who must be purely rational or devoid of feelings, it has been clearly shown that certain feelings play a positive role

---

[8] These conditions have been discussed by Allen Wood (2008), Owen Ware (2009, 2014), Samuel Kahn (2015) and Thomas Hill (2002).

[9] See Carla Bagnoli (2003), Lara Denis (2006) and Maria Borges (2019).

in Kant's moral theory and that they therefore should be cultivated.[10] Some subjective, psychological conditions have rightly been treated as useful tools for maxim observation.

I would like to add my voice to this debate by claiming that we need not presuppose that all helpful psychological conditions must have the same degree of relevance. For example, unlike sympathetic feelings, conscience and moral feelings may also be needed for maxim adoption.[11] I will explain why I hold that moral feeling is required not only for maxim observation but also for maxim adoption and self-determination. Even more importantly for our purposes, if Kant's doctrine of virtue essentially concerns the adoption of particular moral maxims through which the moral law actually moves us to perform morally worthy actions, and if self-control plays a crucial role in this doctrine, it is plausible to assume that self-control also plays a role in the adoption of such maxims.[12] Furthermore, if moral feeling and self-control turn out to be necessary for maxim adoption and ethical end-setting, then our psychological conditions may still be more than a mere means to observing maxims of virtue.

In her valuable book on virtue and autocracy, Anne Margaret Baxley (2010) thoroughly explains the sense in which self-control is needed for following maxims. Along these lines, Paul Guyer (2005: 144) interestingly clarifies how the cultivation of different self-mastery techniques serves as a 'naturally available means' of implementing our maxims. I wish to take here a step further in highlighting the significance of self-control in Kant's theory of virtue.

### 1.2.3 Sketching a New Proposal

I will try to explain the sense in which self-control is needed for setting ourselves moral ends in the process of maxim adoption. Without self-control, there would be no maxims of virtue – the principles that guide us by resulting in morally worthy actions.[13] Kantian maxims exhibit various degrees of

---

[10] See Laura Papish (2007) and Marcia Baron (1995).

[11] Conscience is often addressed only in relation to the actions that we perform in order to follow our maxims. Its role in maxim adoption is hinted at by Guyer (2010: 144) and Timmermann (2006: 303–04). I attempt to highlight this role of Kantian conscience in Vujošević (2014).

[12] By 'moral maxims', I mean morally correct maxims *in abstracto*. Kant discusses the observance of 'moral maxims' or their effectiveness in practice (CPrR 5: 117–18, 153; MM 6: 432).

[13] Robert Louden (2011: 22–23) suggests that self-control is central to virtue but fails to detail why it is necessary for adopting maxims. Louden (2011: 12) takes virtuous maxims to refer to 'underlying intentions and agent's life-plans' and distinguishes them from more specific maxims, conceived of as intentions to perform certain acts. It seems to me that maxims of virtue are rather specific maxims and that we should also explain how such maxims are related to more general ones.

8 *The Philosophy of Immanuel Kant*

generality.[14] For example, the false promise maxim (G 4: 422) seems less general than a 'maxim to act rightly' (MM 6: 231). Like Henry Allison (1990: 93), who explains the relationship between the different kinds of maxims in terms of 'embeddedness', I believe that the idea that maxims come in different degrees of generality does not commit us to the view that more specific maxims of action must be understood as completely separate from the more general ones in which they are 'embedded'.[15] In the *Religion* (6: 20), Kant discusses a common, subjective and ultimate ground of specific maxims, which is itself a maxim. This underlying maxim, exhibiting the moral quality of our character, can be understood as a kind of general commitment either to the moral law or to self-love. It is an agent's disposition that is reflected in her particular choices. I hold that while there is a distinction between particular and underlying maxims, we need not draw it very sharply. As I will explain, Kant gives us reason to hold that our virtuous disposition (*Tugendgesinnung*) serves as the deep subjective ground of our specific maxims. His claim seems to be that we cultivate a virtuous disposition through adopting the more specific moral maxims on which we actually act. The underlying idea is that we continuously renew our general commitment to the moral law by reassessing our incentives and setting particular moral ends in different situations.[16]

My point will be that a renewal of our general commitment to the moral law requires moral strength. In my opinion, Kant's claim about a radical change of heart need not commit us to a merely static view of our disposition.[17] Kant emphasizes that our predisposition to the good gradually becomes our way of thinking: from our own perspective, a reformation of our propensity to evil (as our perverted way of thinking) is gradual because we can judge ourselves and the strength of our maxims only on the basis of our control over sensible impressions (Rel 6: 48).

---

[14] For a survey of different interpretations of maxims see Rob Gressis (2010). My view of maxims comes close to Onora O'Neill's (1989) understanding of maxims as underlying intentions.

[15] Christine Korsgaard (1989) also holds that maxims are arranged hierarchically.

[16] One might still ask whether this works in the case of negatively expressed duties of virtue, for there seems to be no room for ends. For Kant, however, an end need not be an action: 'There can be no will' without 'some end' (TP 8:279), and all virtues entail maxims, which must entail an end (G 4: 436). He accordingly presents inner freedom as the condition of *all* duties of virtue (MM 6: 406). Thus, if an agent is to avoid committing the vice of taking malicious pleasure in intentionally disclosing the faults of others, she must adopt a particular maxim not to degrade others by treating them as mere means to achieving the ends of her inclinations (MM 6: 450). Her maxim should not be based on an inclination to make herself feel better by expressing negative judgements about others. The Kantian virtuous agent ought to compel herself to refrain from disrespecting others by setting the happiness of others as her own end.

[17] As Wood (2020: 89) points out, a change of heart, in time, can only be 'a gradual, open-ended struggle for moral improvement'.

It is not only in this context that Kant speaks of the *strength of maxims* (MM 6: 394; 6: 447; NMM 23: 396). Although it is crucial for explaining virtue as moral strength and moral weakness, this notion remains neglected. Perhaps this is due to a mistaken assumption that Kantian maxims cannot be strong or weak because they are principles. At times, it is simply presupposed that we are always sufficiently motivated to act in accordance with the specific maxims we have, which seems to exclude weakness of will.[18]

Nevertheless, the strength of maxims can be explained by appealing to self-control. Kant suggests that it is by setting aside all sensible impressions that we adopt specific moral maxims that are efficient in practice. It is this aspect of Kant's account of moral self-control that makes it different not only from the Humean view that calm passions control violent ones, but also from the more common view of self-control, according to which reason simply controls passions and feelings. By setting aside all sensible impressions, practical reason (the will) controls itself while adopting virtuous maxims. This aspect of self-control is involved in the free adoption of the particular maxims on which we actually act. Such adoption entails the activity of taking an interest in the action. In my interpretation, the establishment of a pure moral interest is implicit in every particular moral maxim; it is its deep motivating ground, which is to be renewed in different situations. To produce a pure interest by adopting particular moral maxims on this ground, we must make use of our capacity for self-control, by which we are able to set aside all 'impure' incentives.

To be sure, my claim is not that self-control is all that is needed for the adoption of moral maxims. The purely cognitive, theoretical basis of our maxims need not depend on the capacity for self-control. It tells us something about the form of a maxim, which holds 'objectively, i.e., under the idea of a reason having complete control over all subjective moving causes [*subjective Bewegursachen*]' (G 4: 420 n). In other words, self-control is not required for the first element of lawgiving that is tantamount to 'a merely theoretical cognition of a possible determination of choice' (MM 6: 218). But there is also a second element of lawgiving that Kant views as being required for actual self-determination – an incentive that must be included in lawgiving if we are to be motivated to perform an action (MM 6: 218).[19] Without a subjective ground for determining our choices, moral laws would be 'objectively necessitating' for us,

---

[18] Jens Timmermann (2000: 40) seems to hold this view in relation to what he calls 'first-order maxims', conceived of as the subjective principles 'on which we directly act'. Sven Nyholm (2017) criticizes this view.

[19] He states that 'the ground of all practical lawgiving' lies '*objectively in the rule* and the form of universality which makes it fit to be a law', whereas it '*subjectively* ... lies in the *end*' (G 4: 431) [italics in the original].

10 *The Philosophy of Immanuel Kant*

but not 'also at the same time subjectively necessitating' (L-Met 28: 258). We would not be capable of actually determining our choice through adopting maxims of virtue.

My point is that self-control is needed for the second element of lawgiving. It is needed for setting ourselves moral ends. If we are to become morally motivated to perform an action, we must adopt a maxim of virtue by which the moral law becomes an incentive that is powerful enough to move us to perform that action.[20] As Kant suggests, moral laws without incentives are merely objective; they are mere grounds of appraisal that are not at the same time 'subjectively practical' (L-Met 28: 317).[21] Without incentives, our maxims would be mere rules lacking any power to move us to act morally (MM 6: 393). Since moral laws are 'objectively necessitating' for us but not 'also at the same time subjectively necessitating', we ought to adopt maxims through which we *make* the moral law subjectively 'necessitating' (L-Met 28: 258). By adopting maxims of virtue, we make the moral law our own motivationally sufficient incentive. Self-control is required to secure the purity of the subjective motivating ground of our particular maxims, which we renew in different situations by setting ourselves particular moral ends.

Unlike practical laws or imperatives, which are objective practical principles, our morally permissible maxims are subjective principles that 'merely qualify for a giving of universal law' (MM 6: 389). For Kant, a maxim is 'the subjective principle of acting' that 'contains the practical rule determined by reason conformably with the condition of the subject' (G 4: 420–1 n), or a 'rule that the agent himself makes his principle on subjective grounds' (MM 6: 225). Since our maxims are based on 'subjective causes [*subjectiven Ursachen*]', they 'do not of themselves conform with those objective principles' (MM 6: 214). If the objective principles are to serve us 'also subjectively' as practical principles, reason must *gain control* over the faculty of desire (G 4: 401 n). When adopting our own principles of acting, we must also compel ourselves to make the categorical imperative 'subjectively practical'.

Kant therefore provides an account of moral self-control on the basis of which we can argue that Sulla is not virtuous, and is even vicious, because he misuses his capacity for self-control when adopting his maxims. Just like the moral egoist portrayed in the *Anthropology* (7: 130), Sulla starts from the ends that he is anyway eager to adopt, does not constrain himself to adopt moral ends,

---

[20] Feeling respect for the moral law need not suffice for acting virtuously. Although moral self-control presupposes such feelings, it is also necessary for becoming virtuous.

[21] When making this point, Kant also uses the terms 'objectively necessary' and 'subjectively possible' (L-Met 29: 900). In the second *Critique* (5: 151), he writes about reason's sometimes being 'objectively practical' but not also 'subjectively practical'.

## Kant on Self-Control

and adopts maxims to act in accordance with the ends that are objects of his inclinations. As a result, he fails to compel himself to follow morally correct maxims. Even though he forms his own maxims, he fails to freely adopt maxims and to determine his choice in this way. This is why the self-control that he exhibits in disciplining himself to follow his maxims is not moral.

To fully explain Kant's conception of moral self-control, I will interpret it as our ability to '*abstract from*' various sensible impressions. Kant argues that the faculty of *abstraction* 'demonstrates the freedom of the faculty of thought and the authority of the mind, in having the state of one's representations under one's control' (Anth 7: 131, translation modified). When abstracting, we gain control over the state of certain representations in our minds by disregarding the influences of various sensible impressions. Importantly, for Kant, abstraction is an act of paying attention to some of our representations by diverting our attention from others.

My analysis will show that the adoption of maxims of virtue requires that we 'abstract from' all inclinations and the feelings on which they are based, whereas the use of our capacity for self-control to prevent affects and acquired passions would suffice for the mere following of maxims. Controlling ourselves at the level of following maxims need not require that we set aside all natural feelings and inclinations, because some non-affective feelings and some non-passionate inclinations can make maxim observation more efficient.[22]

I will show (i) that Kant's conception of moral self-control necessarily involves two intimately related levels that are meant to meet different criteria, and (ii) that moral self-control, when understood in this way, is central to virtue.

---

[22] I find it important to distinguish between natural inclinations and a different sort of inclination, such as acquired passions, for otherwise we would encroach on our natural desires. Natural inclinations are deeply rooted sensible desires that 'do not have us for their author' (Rel 6: 35). What Kant calls 'an *immediate* inclination' (e.g. G 4: 397) does not yet seem to be directly mediated by a particular maxim. Acquired passions, as I will explain, certainly presuppose the adoption of particular morally impermissible maxims through which we intensify or transform certain natural desires. We intentionally make those natural desires habitual by adopting maxims. Whereas passionate inclinations can be seen as the real enemy of virtue, natural inclinations cannot (Rel 6: 58). And yet, this is not to say that a natural inclination excludes any kind of rationality because it stems only from our animal, non-rational nature. I hold that this would even be impossible on Kant's view, because all our inclinations, unlike those of animals, necessarily include consciousness of our capacity to choose freely, or our capacity for inner freedom. Thus, my view is in general agreement with the stimulating line of thought that questions the separation of our humanity from our animality, suggested by Janelle DeWitt (2018) and Allen Wood (2018). It seems to me that my reading of self-control as abstraction does not start with a kind of dualism in which disregarding our natural desires presupposes a supernatural power that is totally external to those desires. Self-control might be 'a faculty to *do or to refrain from doing as one pleases*' or 'the faculty of desire in accordance with concepts', which is called *choice* when it is 'joined with one's consciousness of the ability to bring about its object by one's action' (MM 6: 213) [italic in the original]. We then also seem responsible when acting out of immediate inclination because we always have this yet-to-be-actualized capacity for self-control or free choice.

12 *The Philosophy of Immanuel Kant*

Although Sulla can be said to have instrumental self-control in the sense of being disciplined enough to follow his immoral maxims, he lacks both levels of moral self-control that are constitutive of virtue. The relevance of self-control, as a psychological condition, goes thus deeper than our mere ability to follow established maxims. Moral self-control is not just an instrument for realizing ends; it is also needed for setting ourselves moral ends. In what follows, I first discuss Kant's notion of autocracy. I then analyse self-control as abstraction and use this analysis to explain Kant's conceptions of moral strength and moral weakness.

## 2 Self-Control through the Lens of 'Autocracy'

Spelling out what Kant means by autocracy is essential to his conceptions of moral self-control and virtue:

> What essentially distinguishes a duty of virtue from a duty of right is that external constraint to the latter kind of duty is morally possible, whereas the former is based only on free self-constraint [*dem freien Selbstzwange*]. – For finite *holy* beings (who could never be tempted to violate duty) there would be no doctrine of virtue but only a doctrine of morals, since the latter is autonomy of practical reason whereas the former is also *autocracy* of practical reason, that is, it involves consciousness of the *capacity* to master one's inclinations when they rebel against the law, a capacity which, though not directly perceived, is yet rightly inferred from the categorical imperative. (MM 6: 383) [italics in the original]

A doctrine of virtue must take into account consciousness of our capacity for self-control.[23] Our moral agency requires the capacity by which we overrule or somehow set aside our sensible impulses. Since ought implies can, we must assume that we have the capacity for self-control. Autocracy is here presented as our consciousness of this capacity – our awareness of being capable of producing certain objects via our choices. It is a specific quality of our practical reason or our will. Without this quality, it would be impossible for us to become virtuous. We must therefore take it into account whenever we address the nature of our moral agency.

Kant has been reported as mentioning 'the autocracy of the mind over all powers of the soul' and 'the autocracy of the human mind and of all the powers of the soul' (L-Eth 27: 364, 368). Autocracy has been treated as the condition of the observance of duties to oneself, and therefore of all other duties. Kant has also been said to explain autocracy in relation to different powers, such as imagination and judgement (L-Eth 27: 365), and to describe autocracy as 'a

---

[23] My discussions in this section draw on Vujošević (2020b).

faculty of keeping' these powers 'under free choice and observation' (L-Eth 27: 364). Furthermore, the Collins and the Mrongovius notes suggest that autocracy is the executive power, which is to be equated with moral feeling (e.g. 27: 361–2; 29: 626).

## 2.1 Different Interpretations of Autocracy

Some scholars claim that autocracy is not a capacity. They argue that it is a matter of being good at exercising different capacities and techniques. Others disagree. On their view, autocracy is the capacity for controlling inclinations. A more substantial disagreement arises when it comes to explaining autocracy's role in acting virtuously in relation to the autonomy–autocracy distinction. Roughly speaking, there are two possibilities. One is to claim that autocracy is only needed to remove obstacles once we are tempted to fail to act in accordance with our already adopted morally correct maxims. The other is to claim that autocracy must also reach deeper than our ability to adhere to our established maxims.

According to Henry Allison's influential reading, autocracy and autonomy are two different aspects of the same capacity. Autocracy is 'actual strength of character or self-control', and autonomy is 'the mere capacity (*Vermögen*) for it' (Allison, 1990: 164). The autonomy–autocracy distinction is cashed out in terms of a capacity and its actualization. Self-control 'is merely a necessary and not also a sufficient condition of virtue', and virtue is a form of self-control that is based on a principle of inner freedom (Allison, 1990: 164). Viewed from this perspective, the vicious Roman dictator Sulla, who is very good at following his morally impermissible maxims, can be said to satisfy a necessary but not also a sufficient condition for virtue. Or, he can be said to lack the form of self-control that characterizes virtue; his self-control is not based on inner freedom and this explains his bad maxims. However, from this we do not yet know whether Sulla should use his capacity for self-control to compel himself to adopt morally permissible maxims and how such self-constraining activity relates to the principle of inner freedom.

A very different explanation of the autonomy–autocracy distinction can be found in Baxley's extensive work on this topic. Baxley (2003: 17–18) finds Allison's reading unsatisfying because it incorrectly 'equates autonomy with a capacity for self-control' and 'fails to capture the legislative-executive thrust of the distinction'. On her view, Allison's reading blurs the distinction between two separate capacities: autonomy as a legislative power and autocracy as an executive power. Autocracy is required for compliance with the norms prescribed by the legislative power of the will, which, as Baxley (2003: 18, 2015:

14 *The Philosophy of Immanuel Kant*

229) adds, involves the notion of self-determination. Accordingly, weakness of the will is explained as a case in which the will is autonomous but has failed to achieve autocracy (Baxley, 2010: 60, 81). Baxley (2003: 15, 16) relatedly claims that autonomy concerns 'motivational independence', whereas autocracy concerns 'temptation independence'.

If viewed in this light, Sulla appears to have a problem with achieving 'motivational independence'. He follows his maxims, and this makes him different from Baxley's weak-willed person who fails to attain 'temptation independence'. Baxley might also argue that Sulla lacks autocracy, understood as a specific kind of self-control that involves following morally correct maxims, that is, a kind of self-control that presupposes autonomy. In any case, according to her 'two separate powers' account, Sulla seems to fail to act virtuously for a completely different reason than a lack of self-control – he somehow, independently of his executive power of self-control, seems to misuse his legislative power.

Paul Guyer (2005) ascribes a similar role to autocracy, but autocracy is not a specific capacity in his view. He argues that the process of achieving autocracy is the empirical realization of autonomy. For Guyer, autonomy is an ideal, and autocracy cannot be the capacity for autonomy when it is realized – it is a state we achieve via the cultivation of different capacities and practices. This cultivation includes strengthening our moral feelings and developing certain techniques, such as controlling our imagination and becoming better at postponing our judgements. Guyer (2005: 143–44) suggests that these different ways of cultivating are 'simply the means' by which we 'implement' maxims or realize moral ends.

Eric Entrican Wilson (2015) finds Guyer's explanation of the autonomy–autocracy distinction unsatisfying because autonomy is a property of the will that we all have. As a result, autocracy cannot be a matter of implementing the ideal of autonomy. Autocracy or 'self-command is a condition or state achieved by those agents who become proficient at solving problems presented by the passions' (Wilson, 2015: 256). Self-command is a matter of being good at exercising different capacities and skills. Such proficiency makes one able to 'stick to the results of self-legislation over time' and to 'extend the results of self-legislation over time' (Wilson, 2015: 256, 271). As a specific kind of moral self-control, self-command presupposes the results of self-legislation.[24] The person with self-command is capable of staying committed to 'the results of his own activity of moral deliberation' (Wilson, 2015: 260).

---

[24] In Wilson's view, self-command is merely an aspect of virtue. He criticizes Allen Wood's claim that self-mastery and virtue are 'equivalent' (Wilson, 2015: 274). I agree with Wilson that his own conception of self-command should not be identified with Kantian virtue.

## Kant on Self-Control

## 2.2 Autocracy Reconsidered

Indeed, Kant does not make it easy to settle the question of whether autocracy is a capacity. In the *Metaphysics of Morals* (6: 383), he argues that autocracy involves consciousness of the capacity to master our inclinations. Elsewhere, he refers to autocracy by using the term 'capacity' (PM 20: 295), and the lecture notes support both the notion that autocracy is to be explained in relation to the exercise of a number of capacities and the notion that autocracy itself is the executive power of self-control. The fact that Kant has been reported as presenting autocracy in relation to other powers, such as imagination and judgement, does not necessarily support the conclusion that autocracy cannot be more closely tied to a particular capacity. The lecture notes suggest that autocracy is not simply about ensuring that we control our inclinations, but also about ensuring that we control all our faculties (L-Eth 27: 364–8; 24: 1496–98). Accordingly, self-control has been described as 'the faculty for freely disposing over the free use of all one's powers' (L-Met 28: 589–90).

What is important for our present purposes, however, and consistent throughout the texts, is that autocracy is inseparable from the capacity for self-control and essential to Kant's conception of virtue. Kant speaks of virtue as an actualized capacity for self-control, but he also holds that we must assume that we always have a mere capacity for self-control (MM 6: 397).[25] Autocracy can then involve consciousness of either our realized or our yet-to-be-realized capacity for self-control. In the lecture notes, autocracy is sometimes used to refer to states in which human beings actually have their inclinations and capacities under control (e.g. L-Eth 29: 626). But it is very unlikely that what Kant had in mind in the passage on autocracy from the *Metaphysics of Morals* (6: 383) was virtue as acquired moral strength. Although there is no doubt that fulfilling duties of virtue requires exercising the capacity for self-control, the doctrine of virtue need not presuppose that we really have our inclinations under control in a given moment, or that we have autocracy as an actual strength. Rather, Kant's suggestion seems to be that autocracy, as a kind of consciousness of the mere capacity for self-control, must be taken into account whenever we want to explain how we can fulfil the duties of virtue.

---

[25] These two aspects of control are also present in the doctrine of right: 'An object of my *choice* is that which I have the physical capacity [*Vermögen*] to use as I please, that whose use lies within my power [*Macht*] (potentia)', which is different from 'having the same object under my control [*Gewalt*] (*in potestatem meam redactum*), which presupposes not merely a *capacity* but also an *act* of choice' (MM 6: 250) [italic in the original]. Something is in my power or is an object of my choice, when I am aware that I *can* control it by using it as I please, that is, when I am aware of having the capacity to do so. But having that object under my control also requires that I exercise this capacity by actually controlling the object. In this case, I must make my choice.

16 *The Philosophy of Immanuel Kant*

At first glance, this claim about autocracy as consciousness of a yet-to-be-actualized capacity for self-control might seem unimportant, or even pointless. But it is not. Kant thought that it is through this consciousness that we become aware of our freedom. Near the end of the second *Critique* (5: 159), he describes how we become aware of our freedom to put the influence of all sensible impressions aside, that is, how we become aware that we *can* do what the moral law demands of us. This is, as Kant illustrates, 'as it were, to raise oneself altogether above the sensible world, and this consciousness of the law also as an incentive is inseparably combined with consciousness of a power of *ruling over sensibility* [*die Sinnlichkeit beherrschenden Vermögens*], even if not always with effect' (CPrR 5: 159) [italic in the original].[26]

An apt illustration of how we become aware of our power to master inclinations is Kant's well-known example in which a prince forces a man to choose between giving a false testimony or being executed. This man 'would perhaps not venture to assert whether he would' really choose to be executed or not, but he 'must admit without hesitation that it is possible for him' to overcome his love of life or to control one of his strongest inclinations (CPrR 5: 30). As soon as he starts forming his maxims, this man becomes conscious of the moral law, and then he also becomes aware that it is *possible* for him to choose to do what the moral law demands. Through his consciousness of his capacity for self-control, he becomes aware that his choice is capable of producing certain objects (MM 6: 213; Anth 7: 251). This seems to be why Kant argues that the capacity for self-control 'can and must be simply *presupposed* in man on account of his freedom' (MM 6: 397).

Even more, the claim that autocracy can be attributed to our will at all times, not only in those moments in which we actually have our inclinations under control, opens up the possibility of self-control's coming into the picture even

---

[26] Before this passage, Kant tries to show that a purely presented morality has 'more power over the human heart' and claims that certain intensive feelings might stimulate but not strengthen the heart (CPrR 5: 156–7). This is in perfect agreement with his other claims about moral strength (e.g. MM 6: 384). He then argues that a dry representation of duty is still more subjectively moving than a consideration of actions that are represented by the inclinations as magnanimous, such as putting oneself in extreme danger in order to rescue people from a shipwreck (CPrR 5: 157–8). When we evaluate the example of a duty to oneself, as Kant continues, 'we give the most perfect esteem to compliance with it at the sacrifice of everything that could ever have value for our dearest inclinations, and we find our soul strengthened and elevated by such an example when we convince ourselves, in it, that human nature is capable of so great an elevation above every incentive that nature can oppose to it' (CPrR 5: 158). Thus, I take Kant to be claiming here that we strengthen our soul by reflecting on examples of duties because that makes us aware of our power to master our inclinations. When it comes to making first-personal moral judgements and adopting one's own maxims, the Kantian moral agent cannot be a moral imitator; he needs to exercise his capacity for self-control in order to set aside the influence of his inclinations on his way of thinking (e.g. CPrR 5: 161). I am grateful to one of the editors for pressing me to further clarify this issue.

during the very process of maxim adoption. Although the man in the above example might be said to have 'a merely theoretical cognition of a possible determination of choice' (MM 6: 218), this knowledge has not yet fed back into his decision regarding how to act in that situation because he has not yet exercised his capacity for self-control by actually refusing to give priority to love of life in his maxim. Drawing on Kant's idea that actual self-determination requires the inclusion of an incentive in lawgiving (MM 6: 218), we may conclude that this man has not yet actually determined his choice. Rather, he has merely realized that it is possible for him to put aside his love of life – he has only become aware of the freedom of his choice.

In line with this, Kant does not seem to draw a clear-cut distinction between autonomy and autocracy by claiming that the latter is only needed for sticking to the results of self-legislation, or for sticking to our already made moral decisions. He claims that the autonomy of practical reason is simultaneously its autocracy (MM 6: 383; PM 20: 295). There are further reasons why I am more willing to accept Allison's explanatory framework than those that present autocracy and autonomy as two completely separate powers. First, it does not seem to rest on a one-sided understanding of Kant's notion of temptation. In the passage from the *Metaphysics of Morals* (6: 383), temptation is mentioned as the reason why autocracy is needed in the case of human beings. Autocracy can be said to be needed because we are tempted not to follow our already adopted, morally good maxims; unlike holy beings who gladly do everything that is in accordance with the moral law, we must compel ourselves to perform morally correct actions. This is acceptable as long as we remember that Kant also holds that purely rational beings are incapable of morally unacceptable maxims (CPrR 5: 32; 5: 79 and G 4: 439) and that we, by contrast, are tempted to adopt such maxims. Acting virtuously involves compelling ourselves to adopt maxims that guide actions that are both morally correct and morally worthy. Given Kant's overall emphasis on the maxims of actions and his insistence that virtue necessarily involves maxims of ends, the main reason why autocracy is needed is rather our temptation to adopt morally impermissible maxims.

Second, the claim that autocracy and autonomy are two separate powers that perform two completely different functions, may find support in the Collins notes (1784–1785) but not in the Mrongovius notes (1785). In both cases, autocracy is presented as the executive power and equated with moral feeling (L-Eth 27: 361–2, 29: 626), but this is glossed in different ways. According to the Collins lecture notes, autocracy is 'the authority to compel the mind', which 'involves mastery over oneself, and not merely the power to direct' (L-Eth 27: 362). This power to direct is a forerunner of autonomy: It corresponds to the principle of appraisal of obligation, which should not be confused with the

18 *The Philosophy of Immanuel Kant*

principle of performance or execution (L-Eth 27: 274–5). The executive power 'can compel us, in spite of all impediments, to produce certain effects' (L-Eth 27: 362). This claim can be taken to suggest that autocracy, as the executive power, is only needed to remove obstacles once we are tempted to fail to act in accordance with our previously made decisions. Compelling ourselves 'to produce certain effects' in spite of all sensible obstacles would then have to be understood as bare compelling ourselves to perform certain physical actions, or as mere disciplining ourselves to obey given rules. If conceived in this way, the capacity for self-control may seem completely different from the power that provides us with norms. However, this conclusion can be challenged by pointing to a passage from the Mrongovius lecture notes that suggests that autocracy involves the self-determination of our reason, rather than simply presupposing it (L-Eth 29: 626). Since the legislative power is meant to involve the notion of self-determination, this causes problems for the reading according to which we should draw a sharp distinction between autocracy and autonomy. Compelling ourselves 'to produce certain effects', then, cannot be reduced to merely disciplining ourselves to follow certain rules.

Furthermore, in the *Metaphysics of Morals*, Kant confirms the intimate relationship between self-determination and moral feeling. Moral feeling is a distinctive kind of pleasure or displeasure that we feel whenever we become aware of our possible morally good or bad actions (MM 6: 399). It is 'respect [*Achtung*]' for the moral law 'in its subjective aspect' (MM 6: 464).[27] Now, Kant's point is that moral feeling is required for self-determination, which is widely held to belong to the legislative power. According to the lecture notes, however, moral feeling is equivalent to autocracy, or the executive power (L-Eth 27: 361–2, 29: 626), and the point that moral feeling is required for self-determination may then be taken to suggest that the executive power's role is not limited to performing physical acts in accordance with the norms issued by the legislative power. In other words, it becomes difficult to defend the claim that autocracy and autonomy are two completely separate powers, and that autocracy only comes into play once the task of self-legislation has been properly fulfilled.

Kant argues that *every determination of choice* proceeds from the representation of a *possible action* through moral feeling (MM 6: 399). This distinctive

---

[27] In the *Metaphysics of Morals*, Kant focuses on this subjective aspect of respect – most prominently in the section on the four subjective conditions of moral receptivity. His choice not to address self-control under the same heading might be taken to reflect his revised view that moral feeling is still not identical to self-control, although they are very closely tied and both can be said to make the moral law practical. As will be explained, moral feelings make us receptive to the concepts of duty, whereas it is through the very activity of self-control that we set ourselves moral ends.

# Kant on Self-Control

19

feeling enables an actual determination of our choice by the moral law, conceived as the state in which we 'take an interest in the action' (MM 6: 399). In line with this, Kant explains that moral laws command morally necessary actions for which

> arises the concept of a duty, observance or transgression of which is indeed connected with a pleasure or displeasure of a distinctive kind (moral *feeling*), although in practical laws of reason we take no account of these feelings (since they have nothing to do with the *basis* of practical laws but only with the subjective *effect* in the mind during the determination of our choice [*bei der Bestimmung unserer Willkür*] [...] (MM 6: 221, translation modified) [italic in the original].

This quotation confirms the thesis that moral feeling is necessary for the determination of our choice by practical laws. It also tells us that moral feeling is not the objective condition of morality that could be the cognitive basis of practical laws. Kant holds that the objective principles cannot be based on any kind of feeling.

However, this does not exclude the possibility that moral feeling, as one of the 'subjective conditions for receptiveness to the concept of duty' (MM 6: 399), is a necessary element in the process of adopting the particular moral maxims on which we actually act. It may still be needed when it comes to the adoption of subjective principles of volition through which we can determine our choice independently of external influences. Together with self-control, which is needed if we are to free ourselves from the influence of sensible impressions on our minds, moral feeling can still be required for the adoption of the rules that we make for ourselves on subjective grounds.

In fact, Kant argues that an incentive is necessarily involved in the maxim adoption characteristic of virtue. In the *Metaphysics of Morals*, he seems to retain the old distinction between the principle of appraisal of obligation and the principle of its execution: now as the difference between a law and an incentive. Whereas the former 'makes an action a duty' by representing it as 'objectively necessary', the latter 'connects a ground for determining choice to this action subjectively with the representation of the law' (MM 6: 218). But Kant now also suggests that every lawgiving must have these two elements and that the second element must be present if we really are to determine our choice (MM 6: 218). An incentive must be included in the process of self-legislation if we are to become morally motivated to perform an action; without a subjective ground for determining our choice, moral laws would never become subjectively practical for us. We would not strongly will what we ought to do, and this is precisely what virtue as moral strength involves.

20     *The Philosophy of Immanuel Kant*

This analysis is of particular importance in explaining the internal law-giving that is constitutive of virtue. Unlike juridical or external lawgiving, internal lawgiving does not allow for inclinations or aversions as determining grounds of our choice. Virtuous lawgiving involves the proper incorporation of the incentive of the duty into the rules we prescribe to ourselves. Neither our own inclinations nor someone else can properly motivate us to act morally, or constrain us to make a free choice in the Kantian sense of determining our choice by the pure incentive. For these purposes, we need to acquire inner freedom. This is why Kant treats inner freedom as the condition of becoming virtuous. In line with this, Kant insists that the way of thinking characteristic of virtue can never become habitual, for virtue would then result from natural necessity. It would be a kind of unfree mechanism. He argues that virtue must always emerge entirely new and original from one's way of thinking (Anth 7: 147) and that the maxims of virtue, which must be freely adopted, are in an unending progression (Anth 7: 147; MM 6: 409; CPrR 5: 32–33).

In order to properly accommodate Kant's claim that virtue must be based on inner freedom and always proceed from freedom, we must also account for self-control in the process of thinking and end-setting. This is how we can explain the specific character of the duties of virtue, or spell out how we, in ever-new situations, determine our choice through the adoption of maxims of virtue. From my point of view, it is very unlikely that Kant's claim is that autocracy, as consciousness of our purely instrumental capacity for self-control, is essential to his doctrine of virtue. Our analysis of self-control through the prism of 'autocracy' shows that it is better not to downgrade Kant's conception of moral self-control to a mere tool for following established rules and sticking to our already made moral choices.

If we read Kantian self-control as abstraction, then we can easily accommodate Kant's essential claims about virtue: because of our temptation to base our maxims on our inclinations and our tendency to self-deception, we must continuously exercise our capacity for abstraction in order to acquire inner freedom, that is, to put aside the influence of all sensible impressions on our minds. In what follows, I will therefore approach self-control as abstraction and explain how this ability can be used to acquire inner freedom.

## 3 Self-Control as Abstraction and Inner Freedom

Kant has been reported to have said that '[v]oluntary abstraction and attention constitutes the principle of self-control [*Selbstbeherrschung*]' (L-Anth 25: 1239). Abstraction is indeed constitutive of Kant's conception of self-control.

## Kant on Self-Control

Further development of this idea reveals different kinds of self-control and clarifies its role in acquiring inner freedom.[28]

### 3.1 Abstraction in Prudential and Moral Self-Control

For Kant, abstraction is essential to prudential self-control. Many people 'are unhappy because they cannot abstract'; the one who plans to get married would have a good marriage if he could 'overlook a wart on his beloved's face' (Anth 7: 131–2). We naturally pay attention to deficiencies, and it takes effort to look away from them or to *abstract from* that sensible representation of a wart. When properly developed, the faculty of abstraction becomes the strength of mind that enables us to set aside the obstacles that stand in the way of our happiness (Anth 7: 132).

The Mrongovius lecture notes (1784–1785) suggest a more nuanced version of this view: not all abstracting is proper (L-Anth 25: 1240). One abstracts too little if one decides against marrying an otherwise perfect woman simply because she has pockmarks, whereas one abstracts too much if one ignores a candidate spouse's beauty and allows fear of infidelity to determine one's choice; both end up unhappy, because they do not abstract *at will* (L-Anth 25: 1240). They involuntarily follow the natural flow of their attention. If they were to abstract voluntarily, they would exhibit self-control and manage to make themselves happy (L-Anth 25: 1239).

This kind of self-control is in accordance with the rules of prudence (L-Eth 27: 362). It is in the service of the human general desire for happiness. Of course, claiming that prudential self-control involves abstracting from our general inclination toward happiness or from all particular inclinations the satisfaction of which promotes our happiness, would make prudential self-control pointless. Kant's claim cannot be that one acquires prudential self-control by abstracting from one's desire to enjoy deserved leisure or a good meal and companionship; such desires are even in line with 'the law of virtue' and make virtue appealing.[29]

By Kant's lights, only feelings and desires that make us lose self-control are obstacles to promoting our happiness, and we can use our ability to *abstract from* different sensible impressions to avoid such feelings and desires. Kant thought that having affects and passions is imprudent (Anth 7: 253, 267, 273). His example of a rich person 'whose servant clumsily breaks a beautiful and rare crystal goblet' (Anth 7: 254) illustrates the use of abstraction in preventing

---

[28] Discussions in this section draw significantly on my account of the Kantian capacity for self-control (Vujošević, 2020b).

[29] See Anth 7: 276–80 and 7: 282. I am indebted to one of the editors of this volume for this point.

22    *The Philosophy of Immanuel Kant*

affects. The underlying thought is that it is possible for the rich man to avoid becoming overpowered by his anger. If he were to make a quick 'calculation in thought' and compare the pain he feels as a reaction to the accident to all the pleasures he enjoys as a rich man, he would not fear the loss of his entire happiness and would not descend into the affective state of anger. Gaining control over the condition of the representations in his mind by abstracting from the representation of his broken crystal goblet might prevent him from entering into an affective state in which he is no longer capable of comparing one feeling against the sum of other feelings. Kant analogously presents the imprudence of passions: When in a passionate state, we are no longer capable of comparing one desire with the sum of all other desires (Anth 7: 265). When making a choice, a person with a passion for avarice becomes blind to all other desires, such as her desire to be loved by others. Together with the insatiability of the passions (Anth 7: 266), this makes this person unhappy.[30]

And yet, Kant's view is not that we merely use our capacity for abstraction in order to realize the ends we necessarily have, such as our happiness. This capacity can also be used in more complex cases where we ought to set ourselves certain ends and realize them. Many passages are suggestive of this, but the following seems most telling:

> [T]he human being is not thereby required to *renounce* his natural end, happiness, when it is a matter of complying with his duty; for that he cannot do, just as no finite rational being whatever can; instead, he must *abstract* altogether from this consideration when the command of duty arises; he must on no account make it the *condition* of his compliance with the law prescribed to him by reason; indeed he must, as far as is possible for him, strive to become aware that no *incentive* derived from that gets mixed, unnoticed, into the determination of duty, .... (TP 8: 278–9) [italic in the original].[31]

Since none of our inclinations should determine our maxim adoption, we must *abstract from* all inclinations when adopting virtuous maxims. This does not involve banishing inclinations from our minds. We cannot and should not get rid of our inclinations.[32] Abstracting from all inclinations, or redirecting our attention from them, is required if we are to take an interest in compliance with the moral law and set ourselves moral ends. When we exercise our capacity for abstraction in accordance with the categorical imperative – with the aim of properly incorporating the incentive of the moral law into our maxims – our use of this capacity is called moral.

---

[30] I explain how we use abstraction to prevent passions in 3.3.2.

[31] See also: G 4: 441, CPrR 5: 118 and CJ 5: 294.

[32] Our picture of human nature should be more realistic than that held by the Stoics (Rel 6: 58n); we need not presuppose that we really can take up the position of God.

## Kant on Self-Control

Thus far, we know that abstraction can be voluntary and involuntary, and that voluntary abstraction, which is crucial for self-control, is opposed to our natural way of paying attention. However, Kant does not deny the intimate relationship between abstraction and attention. As his students' notes suggest: 'the same attention is present in abstraction, only the objects are different' (L-Anth 25: 1239); attention does 'not stop with abstraction', and abstraction 'is the actualization of attention' (L-Met 29: 878). Abstraction is a more complex attentive activity. In the *Attempt to Introduce the Concept of Negative Magnitudes into Philosophy* (2: 190), Kant claims that abstraction can be called 'negative attention' because it is an effort to cancel 'certain clear representations' for the purposes of ensuring that what remains becomes 'much more clearly represented'. Abstraction involves an effort to disregard certain representations and redirect our attention to others so that they become more clear. It can be said to involve attention, but not the attention that we naturally pay to sensible objects.

In his *Anthropology* (7: 131), Kant argues that abstraction consists neither in merely paying attention nor in a lack of attentiveness. Attention and abstraction are different ways of becoming conscious of certain representations. When abstracting, we are not simply distracted by something – we voluntarily pay attention to some of our representations by turning attention away from others. For Kant, abstraction is 'a real act of the cognitive faculty of stopping a representation of which I am conscious from being in connection with other representations' (Anth 7: 131). It is a cognitive act through which we intentionally sever the relation between certain representations in our minds with the aim of focusing our attention on something else. Kant further reveals what he means by abstraction:

> To be able to abstract from a representation, even when the senses force it on a person, is a far greater faculty than that of paying attention to a representation, because it demonstrates the freedom of the faculty of thought and the authority of the mind, in having the state [*Zustand*] of one's representations under one's control (*animus sui compos*). (Anth 7: 131; translation modified)

The faculty of abstraction enables us to oppose natural necessity by ignoring representations of the sensible objects we encounter. We actually abstract from 'a determination of the object', as it were, incorporated in our representation (Anth 7: 131). When abstracting, we disregard the determinations that the sensible objects impose on us, and we do so by *modifying the status* of the representations of these objects in our consciousness. We cannot really banish such representations from our minds, but what we can do is *gain control* over

24 *The Philosophy of Immanuel Kant*

their *state* in our minds by disregarding the influence of various sensible impressions. Our capacity for abstraction makes us capable of reasoning as if the sensible impressions that we receive from objects did not exist in our minds.[33]

In sum, abstraction is the cognitive activity of preventing the influence of various sensible objects on our consciousness by redirecting our attention from them in order to pay better attention to the representations that remain. As such, it need not only have the negative aim of disengaging from certain representations. In what follows, I will explain this by showing how Kant's notion of abstraction helps us to get a better grip on his view of self-control, inner freedom and self-determination. Before doing so, however, I will sketch the rudimentary level of self-control needed for mental health.

## 3.2 The Elementary Level of Self-Control

Kant argues that abstraction should not be reduced to distraction (Anth 7: 131), but he sometimes also treats distraction as a kind of abstraction. He claims that distraction (*Zerstreuung*) is 'the state of diverting attention (*abstractio*) away from certain ruling representations [*Vorstellungen*] by dispersing it among other, dissimilar ones' (Anth 7: 206; translation modified). Distraction can be either involuntary or voluntary (Anth 7: 206). Involuntary distraction is absent-mindedness. Voluntary distraction or dissipation involves intentionally taking one's mind off things, thereby creating a diversion from one's 'involuntary reproductive power of imagination' (Anth 7: 206–7). With voluntary distraction we intentionally redirect our attention, but we do so without having the aim of paying better attention to the representations that remain. For example, when trying to get 'rid of the object' that makes us feel sad (L-Anth 25: 1240) we divert our attention from the representations that our recalcitrant power of imagination continuously reproduces, and we do so by dispersing attention to some other objects – for instance, by occupying ourselves 'fleetingly with diverse objects in society' (L-Anth 25: 1240).

Voluntary distraction is a precondition of mental health (Anth 7: 207). Kant's discussion of hypochondria explains why voluntary distraction is an elementary level of self-control and how self-control is related to some other capacities. Picture someone who interprets every little sniff and cough as a sign of a serious

---

[33] In *On a Discovery* (8: 200n), Kant writes that a philosopher 'abstracts *from* that which he does not wish to take into account in a certain use of the concept'. Elsewhere, he suggests that pure moral concepts *abstract from* what is sensitive but are not themselves 'abstracted from everything sensitive' (ID 2: 395). Unlike empirical concepts, they cannot be acquired through induction or abstracted from the input of sensibility. Rather, the concepts of duty abstract from sensible representations by setting them aside.

disease and who suffers from obsessive fear and anxiety as a result. We can apply Kant's insights to this case. This person is involuntarily distracted – he clings to certain representations so strongly that he cannot let them go, and he is in an unhealthy state in which he lacks self-control (L-Anth 25: 1240). True, his condition is not as severe as madness, where 'fantasy plays completely with the human being and the unfortunate victim has no control at all over the course of his representations' (Anth 7: 181). Still, he cannot freely use his capacities for imagination, reason and feeling. Hypochondriacs have a diseased imagination (*Einbildungskrankheit*) (Anth 7: 213). The imagination of the person in question turns into mere fantasy because he cannot restrain its play at will. As a mere quasi-mechanical activity, his imagination regularly misinterprets certain physical sensations as the symptoms of disease. He cannot intentionally turn his attention away from every little sniff and cough and refrain from seeing them as harbingers of doom. Moreover, he cannot help thinking that he has a serious disease, although he might at times realize that this is an irrational belief to hold. In the case of hypochondria, 'the patient is aware that something is not going right with the course of his thoughts, insofar as his reason has insufficient control over itself, to direct, stop or impel the course of his thoughts' (Anth 7: 202). Furthermore, his obsessive fear and anxiety are the signs of his hypochondria, which is the opposite of the mind's power to master ill feelings (CF 7: 103). In sum, he cannot voluntarily distract himself from the chimerical representations that the reproductive power of the imagination unrestrainedly produces; his reason cannot control itself by disregarding the influence of certain sensible impressions, and he cannot free himself from the ill feelings elicited by the figments of his imagination. This lack of control over his own capacities destroys the balance of the soul necessary for his mental health.

The capacity for abstraction in this elementary form, conceived as a certain degree of control over the course of one's sensible representations, is not only a prerequisite for mental health. It is also a precondition for exercising self-control on a higher level that is more directly required for the fulfilment of one's moral obligations. Kant states that being subjected to affects and passions is 'probably always an illness of the mind' (Anth 7: 251), and he describes moral strength of soul as a state of health in moral life (MM 6: 409; 6: 384). As in the case of mental health, when Kant speaks of virtue as moral strength he seems to have in mind a balance of the soul that involves having control over all its powers. I will examine how we acquire the inner freedom of virtue by exercising our capacity for self-control: first as preventing affects and acquired passions, then as abstracting from other inclinations and feelings on which they are based.

## 3.3 Acquiring Inner Freedom

Defining virtue merely as self-constraint does not capture its essence: Virtue would then be a battle of our inclinations in which the stronger inclination wins. It must be free self-constraint (MM 6: 383). Kant therefore discusses virtue as 'self-constraint in accordance with a principle of inner freedom' and as 'a moral constraint', which is possible 'in accordance with the laws of inner freedom' (MM 6: 394; 6: 405). Inner freedom is the constitutive basis of virtue, and it is inseparable from self-control:

> Since virtue is based on inner freedom it contains a positive command to a human being, namely to bring all his capacities and inclinations under his (reason's) control and so to rule over himself [*Herrschaft über sich selbst*], which goes beyond forbidding him to let himself be governed by his feelings and inclinations (the duty of *apathy*); for unless reason holds the reins of government [*die Zügel der Regierung*] in its own hands, his feelings and inclinations play the master over him. (MM 6: 408) [italic in the original]

Inner freedom is 'the condition of all duties of virtue' (MM 6: 406). In the first instance, it is this condition merely in a negative sense – as a way of dealing with our inner obstacles to morality.[34] Acquiring inner freedom is necessary for becoming virtuous, because removing outer obstacles would only suffice for acting in accordance with duty and the fulfilment of duties of right. With regard to duties of right, it does not matter whether the end that one intends is moral, or whether one's maxim is genuinely moral. By contrast, if the moral agent is to act for the sake of duty, she must set herself moral ends, which requires that she fulfils the duty of apathy.

The above quotation also suggests that inner freedom surpasses the fulfilment of the duty of apathy. Inner freedom is also the condition of virtue in a positive sense. It entails a positive command that human beings rule or control themselves. By holding 'the reins of government in its own hands', or by governing our feelings and desires, our reason prevents them from mastering us. As I will clarify, this self-government or self-rule is self-determination. The virtuous way of thinking is one by which we freely determine ourselves 'to act through the thought of the law' (MM 6: 407). What matters here is the way in which agents determine their choices: Kantian virtuous agents must freely adopt their maxims, and not because of the feelings and desires they happen to have. Such agents must set themselves moral ends. They must redirect their attention to these 'pure' ends.

---

[34] I agree with Stephen Engstrom (2002: 304) that Kant uses the term 'inner freedom' to denote both a capacity and its realization.

## Kant on Self-Control

In the *Metaphysics of Morals*, Kant discusses two requirements of inner freedom (MM 6: 407): freedom with regard to affects and freedom with regard to passions. These requirements represent different aspects of the capacity for self-control.[35] Even more, I take Kant to be suggesting that there is also a third requirement of inner freedom, which involves the crucial, but neglected aspect of moral self-control. Here, I have in mind Kant's claim that inner freedom is the capacity to release ourselves from *all* inclinations and corresponding feelings (CPrR 5: 161).

In what follows, I analyse these three requirements of inner freedom as aspects of self-control, conceived as abstraction.[36] My analysis shows that the use of the capacity for self-control to prevent affects and passions, which would suffice for following maxims of virtue, serves as a kind of preparatory ground for their adoption, whereas the actual adoption of these maxims also requires that we set aside all inclinations and the feelings on which they are based. On this basis, I conclude that Kant's conception of moral self-control necessarily involves two intimately related levels, and that it can be central to virtue only if understood in this way.

### 3.3.1 The First Requirement of Inner Freedom

In the first place, inner freedom requires that one tames one's affects and becomes 'one's own master [*Meister*] in a given case (*animus sui compos*)' (MM 6: 407). Affects are brief feelings of pleasure and displeasure that make us lose our composure. An affect is a 'surprise through sensation [*Überraschung durch Empfindung*]' (Anth 7: 252). Such surprises temporarily bring us into a state in which we do not possess ourselves or determine our actions by free choice (L-Eth 27: 626). Once we find ourselves in an affective state, our powers seem to be paralyzed – in those very moments, we can hardly regain control over them. We are not our own masters in the sense that the first requirement of inner freedom demands.

Given that we can hardly control our affects when in an affective state, we might wonder what Kant's taming of the affects could possibly mean. He also argues that we have a duty to ensure that we are free of affects and that our minds are capable of governing them (MM 6: 408; Anth 7: 253). This

---

[35] On the contrary, Ina Goy (2013: 184, 203) argues that two completely different capacities are in question. In Engstrom's view (2002: 310), the two requirements are 'quite different in character': the function of the first is cultivation, whereas the function of the second is the correcting function of self-discipline. As will become clear, I believe the textual evidence supports a different account.

[36] This will also clarify why I disagree with accounts that reduce autocracy to a kind of proficiency needed to solve the problems presented by the passions.

28 *The Philosophy of Immanuel Kant*

government (*Regierung*) must take place before we are gripped by affects. As the Mrongovius notes on anthropology (25: 1342) suggest, we are not blameworthy when in an affective state, but we are blameworthy for letting ourselves fall into that state. Kant's point can hardly be that we ought to acquire inner freedom by setting aside the very affect that holds sway over us. Rather, we should avoid descending into affective states by taking care not to allow our feelings to turn into intense feelings that overpower us. For example, when in the affective state of anger, we can no longer redirect our attention, but we can try to avoid falling into an affective state by redirecting our attention or by abstracting from certain sensible representations before being gripped by the affect.

When discussing the Stoic principle of apathy, Kant explains that the wise man must not even be in a state of affective compassion with the misfortune of his best friend (Anth 7: 253). Such an affect would render him momentarily incapable of using his powers to help his friend. Even more, a compassionate affective state would temporarily hinder his reflective abilities. Affects render the mind 'incapable of engaging in free consideration [*Überlegung*] of principles [*Grundsätze*], in order to determine itself in accordance with them' (CJ 5: 272). Hence, affective compassion would render him not only momentarily incapable of following his maxims, but also incapable of freely using his power of reflection, which is necessary for adopting maxims of virtue. This is why he should ensure that his feelings do not turn into affects.

We must turn to the faculty of abstraction in order to explain how we fulfil the duty of apathy.[37] This faculty is needed to prevent the strong impact that affects can have on our thoughts and actions. For instance, we can take care to ensure that our natural sympathetic feelings do not become affects by disregarding the sensible impressions that would otherwise make them so intense as to overpower us. We can try to abstract from the representation of blood, for instance, if such a representation will paralyze our powers and prevent us from helping someone in need.

This is not to say that we should somehow discard our natural compassionate feelings. We have an indirect duty to cultivate these feelings in order to use them as means for active and rational benevolence, which is based on moral principles (MM 6: 457). As I will explain in the next section, approaching self-control as abstraction also sheds new light on Kant's notion of cultivation. For

---

[37] Kant describes apathy as the absence of affects (Anth 7: 253; CJ 5: 272). In his discussion of apathy in the doctrine of virtue, he contrasts health in moral life with all sorts of affects, including those aroused by the thought of what is good (MM 6: 409). Elsewhere, he seems to suggest that affects stimulated by reason, such as astonishment at unexpected wisdom (Anth 7: 261), genuine moral courage (Anth 7: 257) and enthusiasm (Anth 7: 269, CJ 5: 271), should not be prevented.

now, it is important to note that the first requirement of inner freedom involves the prevention of affects – those feelings that cannot serve us as means for the observance and adoption of maxims of virtue. Generally, affects make us incapable of controlling our actions and bring us out of the state in which cool reflection is possible.[38] Being free of affects is therefore necessary for both voluntary actions and adopting maxims. To be virtuous – to have moral maxims and to act accordingly – we ought to avoid descending into affective states by setting aside various sensible impressions. This is how we disable the influence of sensible impressions that would otherwise bring us out of the calm state of mind in which we can freely employ our powers.

### 3.3.2 The Second Requirement of Inner Freedom

Inner freedom also requires ruling oneself (*über sich selbst Herr zu sein*) or controlling (*beherrschen*) one's own passions (MM 6: 407). This second requirement of inner freedom obliges us to do our best not to become enslaved by passions – those inclinations that 'can be conquered only with difficulty or not at all' (Anth 7: 251). Inclinations are habitual or sensible desires, and passions are powerful, long-lasting inclinations (MM 4: 608). For example, hatred is a kind of lasting passionate desire that involves certain feelings (MM 4: 608). Like other sensible desires, passions are preceded by and based on feelings (MM 6: 211–14).

In this context, Kant likely has in mind acquired passions (Anth 7: 267). Such passions are sensible desires that we also make habitual through setting ourselves certain rules (Anth 7: 267–8). We have 'an interest of inclination' when we make the connection between our feeling of pleasure and the corresponding desire a general rule for ourselves (MM 6: 212). Acquired passions are based on a maxim established for the end prescribed by an inclination (Anth 7: 266).

One may still object that this explanation does not suffice for specifying passionate desires. What interests us and determines our desire in the case of non-passionate inclinations is also an object insofar as it is agreeable to us, and we base our maxims on the ends of such inclinations. Just like passions, other inclinations can be based on maxims in which evil is taken up as something intentional (MM 6: 408). Yet we seem to acquire passions by intensifying a natural inclination that is directed at human beings, through laying down a general rule that our desire be persistently dependent on a certain object because of that inclination. Kant emphasizes that passions are insatiable

---

[38] Kant usually claims that affects preclude reflection, but he sometimes also suggests that they only make reflection more difficult (MM 6: 407).

(Anth 7: 266). Furthermore, a passionate person makes it a rule for himself to act in a way that allows him to achieve the end that is determined by one of his inclinations, and he aims merely to possess the means for satisfying all inclinations that are directly concerned with that end (Anth 7: 270). This need not hold for all morally impermissible maxims. The maxim of falsely promising to pay back money in order to get oneself out of trouble (G 4: 422) need not presuppose a readiness to employ all possible means to reach the end of obtaining money. A maxim on which passions are based would instead be something like: 'In order to be able to dominate others, I make it my principle to increase my wealth by any means'.[39] Acquiring passions involves adopting specific morally incorrect maxims and being motivated to follow them at any cost. The latter need not hold for non-passionate inclinations. Freeing ourselves of passions facilitates the observance of our maxims, but this need not hold for the inclination to help, so long as it does not turn into a passion (CPrR 5: 118; Anth 7: 267).

Having passions is also morally reprehensible because passions make the adoption of virtuous maxims or 'all determinability of choice by means of principles [*Grundsätze*] difficult or impossible' (CJ 5: 272 n; translation modified). By improperly using our reasoning ability when acquiring passions, we distort our reflection at its very root, both morally and prudentially. By determining our choice by means of morally incorrect maxims (described above) we intensify one of our natural inclinations, which becomes so powerful that we can hardly control its influence on our way of thinking and judging. We come to see everything merely in light of that desire and its empirical end.[40] As Kant explains, we put ourselves in a state in which we are no longer able to compare that inclination with the sum of all other inclinations (Anth 7: 265). These chains that we put on our thinking and judging can be removed only with great difficulty, if at all. Kant leaves open whether it is very difficult or impossible to free ourselves of passions once we have them (e.g. Anth 7: 251, 7: 266 and CJ 5: 272 n).

It is therefore not clear that we can get rid of passions once we have acquired them. Given that 'ought' does not seem to imply 'can' in these cases, Kant's second requirement of inner freedom instead involves the prevention of passions. As the Powalski lecture notes suggest, we prevent passions by 'nipping them in the bud [*in ihrem Keime erstikken*]' (27: 207).

---

[39] The first part of this maxim is necessary because Kant emphasizes that passions are inclinations directed towards human beings (Anth 7: 270).

[40] Since Kant points out that passions 'can even co-exist with rationalizing' (Anth 7: 265), I agree with Wehofsits (2020: 1207) to the extent that some passions involve what she calls 'impassioned self-deception'.

We can explain this process by turning to our capacity for abstraction.[41] Kant argues that passion for domination starts from a fear of being dominated by others; this feeling turns into the intention of 'placing the advantage of force on them', which is an imprudent and 'unjust means of using other human beings for one's own purposes' (Anth 7: 273). Our fear of domination leads us to adopt a maxim of dominating others: We make it our principle to use others as a means of dealing with our own unpleasant feelings. In order to prevent this, we should avoid basing our desires on feelings of fear, and we can do so by disregarding their influence on our way of thinking. The same holds for the passion of vengeance, although Kant takes us to acquire this passion in a different way. He argues that the passion of vengeance arises when we suffer an injustice and then transform our permissible desire for justice into a strong and violent desire to do anything we can, even at great personal cost, to harm the one who has been unjust to us (Anth 7: 270–1). Instead of directing our hatred at injustice, we direct it at the offender, transforming our desire for justice by adopting a morally impermissible maxim of seeking to harm or destroy him by all means possible. This can be prevented by exercising control over the condition of certain representations in our minds. Such transformations of our otherwise permissible desire for fairness can be avoided by ignoring the feelings and desires we happen to have towards the one who has treated us unfairly; this is how we can prevent them from determining our choice, or how we can avoid adopting a maxim of revenge.

To fully explain how we can prevent passions from forming, however, we must turn to another requirement of inner freedom. The above discussion suggests that we should acknowledge the role of self-control in facilitating maxim adoption, whereas the analysis of the third requirement shows that self-control is directly involved in the adoption of maxims of virtue.

### 3.3.3 The Third Requirement of Inner Freedom

In the second *Critique*, Kant writes that inner freedom is the capacity to release (*losmachen*) ourselves from 'inclinations, so that none of them, not even the dearest, has any influence on a decision [*Entschließung*] for which we are now to make use of our reason' (5: 161). This requirement of inner freedom entails setting aside all inclinations and the feelings on which they are based. As deeply rooted sensible desires, inclinations are sensible incentives through which the

---

[41] This is not to say that conscience is not needed. Conscience has to do with honesty with ourselves in 'screening incentives' (Rel 6: 37); it is necessary for self-cognition and maxim adoption, especially because of our deep-seated tendency to self-deception. By exercising our capacity for self-control in accordance with the moral law, we set aside 'impure' incentives and set ourselves moral ends.

32                    *The Philosophy of Immanuel Kant*

object of our desire determines our power of choice (Rel 6: 21). When it comes to making moral decisions and considering which maxims we are to adopt, none of our inclinations may determine our way of thinking. Autonomous lawgiving does not allow for sensible incentives: heteronomy results whenever we let our choices be determined by inclinations and aversions, or 'pathological' determining grounds.

This is not to say that we can and should rid ourselves of our inclinations (CPrR 5: 84 and 5: 117). Rather, we should bracket their influence on our minds or act as if they did not exist, thereby preventing them from becoming our main incentives for adopting maxims. We must, as Kant explains, '*abstract from* all objects to this extent: that they have no *influence* at all on the will, so that practical reason (the will) may not merely administer an interest not belonging to it, but may simply show its own commanding authority as supreme lawgiving' (G 4: 441) [italic added for emphasis].

In a similar vein: '[R]eason must not play the part of mere guardian to inclination but, disregarding it altogether [*ohne auf sie Rücksicht zu nehmen*], must attend solely to its own interest as pure practical reason' (CPrR 5: 118). Were the interest based on inclinations sufficient for Kantian moral agency, our reason would only govern us by deciding which of our inclinations to fulfil. However, this represents a Humean picture of practical reason and moral agency. On a Kantian picture, practical reason is not merely instrumental and moral ends are not simply given to us by our desires: Virtue involves setting ourselves moral ends and taking a different kind of interest. It requires a pure moral interest – the interest produced by 'freeing ourselves from' all inclinations and corresponding feelings. Taking an interest in moral ends requires such purifying activity, whereas having the interest of inclination does not. To perform a morally worthy action, we must take an interest in moral ends, and we do so by adopting maxims of virtue or maxims of ends. We must compel ourselves to make the formal principle of duty our own principle of acting, and we can do so by redirecting our attention from the ends of inclinations to moral ends.

Relatedly, Kant clarifies that the constraining power of the moral law 'actually makes itself aesthetically knowable only through sacrifices (which is a deprivation, although in behalf of inner freedom, but also reveals in us an unfathomable depth of this supersensible faculty . . .' (CJ 5: 271). He continues by explaining that in the case of a pure moral interest 'the satisfaction on the aesthetic side (in relation to sensibility) is negative, i.e., contrary to this interest, but considered from the intellectual side it is positive' (CJ 5: 271). The feelings that accompany the constraining power of the moral law and 'make moral aversion sensible', such as disgust and horror (MM 6: 406), seem to be our initial reaction to the requirements of the moral law.[42] As Kant also suggests, such emotional reactions are 'an aesthetic device' that 'points to a moral sense' – by that time rejected by him as the source of our moral knowledge – and this device helps us 'to get the better of *merely* sensible incitements' (MM 6: 406). According to the third requirement of inner freedom, none of our inclinations and the feelings on which they are based may determine our moral judgements.[43]

Importantly, this interpretation suggests that the role of self-control, interpreted as the capacity for abstraction, is not merely negative. Kant's idea that abstraction can be understood as a sort of attention is in keeping with his claim that reason 'must attend [*besorgen*] solely to its own interest as pure practical reason' (CPrR 5: 118). Abstraction, as a kind of actualized attention, might be seen as this attending and its function does not end once we have forbidden ourselves to be governed by our inclinations.

We must even continuously exercise our capacity for abstraction to set aside all our inclinations and the feelings on which they are grounded. We can never be completely independent of inclinations and needs in the way that a supreme being is or would be (CPrR 5: 118), but we have a duty to achieve this independence by disregarding the influence of sensible impressions on our minds. As will be elaborated in the next section, Kant emphasizes that maxims of virtue must always be freely adopted, and we have reason to claim that the establishment of a pure moral interest, as our virtuous disposition, is implicit in maxims of virtue by being their deep motivating ground. This ground can be seen as our general commitment to the moral law, which is to be renewed by reassessing our incentives in different situations.

Kant's point is still not that we become morally motivated in the absence of desires and feelings, for there are desires and feelings that are triggered by the moral law and pure reason. The Kantian duty of apathy does not require a state of moral indifference in which we lack desires and feelings altogether: Apathy should not be conceived as 'subjective indifference [*Gleichgültigkeit*] with respect to objects of choice' (MM 6: 408). This duty certainly does not demand that we disregard our moral feelings. As a subjective condition of virtue, moral feeling must be present. There is a '*moral* interest' – 'a pure sense-free interest

---

[42] Horror, as a degree of fear (Anth 7: 256), also appears to play a role in Kant's descriptions of conscience. For instance, he claims that every human being 'finds himself observed, threatened and kept in awe (respect coupled with fear) by an internal judge' (MM 6: 438). And yet, the 'fearful voice' (MM 6: 438) of conscience does not yet seem to be the Kantian moral motive. Kantian conscience, as moral self-appraisal, instead participates in the process of moral motivation by approving and disapproving incentives (L-Met 29: 900).

[43] As I will explain shortly, this is not to say that such feelings and corresponding inclinations should be disregarded at the level of self-control associated with mere maxim observation.

34 *The Philosophy of Immanuel Kant*

of practical reason alone', and moral feeling is 'the capacity to take such an interest in the law' (CPrR 5: 79–80). As explained, moral feeling makes the adoption of maxims of virtue possible; it facilitates the determination of choice by practical laws and does so by being an incentive. Kant holds that pure incentives, as subjective determining grounds, are necessary for the actual determination of our choice by moral laws. Without this element of lawgiving and self-control, maxims of virtue would never actually lead to action. Self-control, understood as abstraction from all inclinations and corresponding feelings, is involved in the free adoption of the particular maxims on which we actually act. It is through exercising our capacity for self-control that we deal with the temptation to adopt our maxims because of our inclinations.[44]

Kant also argues that virtue, since it is based on inner freedom, surpasses the duty of apathy by containing the positive command of *self-rule* (MM 6: 408). This self-rule consists in setting aside all inclinations, but it is simultaneously the rule over all other capacities – including reason itself. By setting aside all sensible impressions, we constrain our way of thinking while adopting maxims of virtue. This is what is meant by self-determination. By setting aside the influence of sensible impressions, reason determines choice 'independently of sensory impulses, thus through motives [*Bewegursachen*] that can only be represented by reason' (CPR A 801/B 829).

This self-rule, conceived as self-determination, is precisely the kind of self-control that the cruel Roman dictator Sulla lacks. He fails to meet the requirement of setting aside all inclinations and the feelings on which they are based. That is, he fails to meet the condition of virtue – the acquisition of inner freedom through exercising the specific kind of self-control required for virtuous end-setting. Even though he forms his own maxims, Sulla fails to freely adopt morally permissible maxims and to determine his choice in this way. He cannot be said to exercise free self-constraint, because he starts from the ends that he is anyway eager to adopt. This is why the self-control that he exhibits in disciplining himself to follow his maxims is merely instrumental and not yet moral. He therefore lacks both levels of moral self-control.

The above analysis of the capacity for self-control as abstraction shows that Kant's conception of moral self-control involves two intimately related levels that are constitutive of virtue and need not meet the same criteria. One level is associated with setting moral ends, the other with realizing various ends. Furthermore, whereas one level is connected to our ability to freely adopt maxims of virtue and requires that we abstract from all inclinations and corresponding feelings, the other is associated with our mere ability to act in

---

[44] Temptation in this sense is the main reason why we need autocracy.

accordance with these maxims and does not necessarily require this radical abstraction.

Controlling ourselves at the level of following maxims need not require that we disregard all inclinations and the feelings on which they are based. Feelings of aversion that accompany the constraining power of the moral law 'make its efficacy felt' (MM 6: 406). Some other feelings, such as sympathetic feelings, should even be cultivated, and certain non-passionate inclinations can make maxim observation more efficient. For example, Kant does not exclude the possibility that one's natural inclination to help might 'facilitate the effectiveness of *moral* maxims' although it cannot produce a moral maxim (CPrR 5: 118). As long as we do not let such inclinations become our main incentives for the adoption of our maxims, they can help us to realize our moral ends. Acting from duty is giving priority to the incentive of the moral law, rather than unsuccessfully trying to destroy all cooperating inclinations. Roughly speaking, when agents are not in an affective or passionate state, their prudential and instrumental self-control can prove useful for realizing their moral ends.

On the other hand, adopting maxims of virtue requires that we acquire inner freedom by setting aside all inclinations and corresponding feelings – that we abstract from all sensible impressions. Self-control, at this level, is not only about facilitating maxim adoption by preventing affects and passions; it is also involved in the very process of adopting virtuous maxims of ends. The actualization of our capacity for self-control at this level is actual self-determination, and this is why self-control is central to virtue.

## 4 A Twofold Account of Moral Strength

Many would agree that it is implausible to attribute moral strength and virtue to Sulla. Some might think that strength enters the picture only once Sulla has adopted his maxims. Strength of soul can be called moral because it presupposes morally permissible maxims – the adoption of which has nothing to do with strength or self-control. But Kant seems to suggest a different picture. The person who commits a crime is a plaything of his natural impulses: 'The basis of great crimes is merely the force of inclinations that weaken reason, which proves no strength of soul' (MM 6: 384). Various sensible influences hold sway over that person's way of thinking such that he does not freely employ his reasoning capacity. Sulla's lack of moral strength may then also explain his improper maxim adoption.[45]

---

[45] This is not to say that Sulla merely lacks moral strength, as the weak-willed agent does. Rather, moral weakness is the first, but necessary stage of Sulla's viciousness. He also misuses his capacity for moral self-control when setting himself immoral ends.

The underlying assumption of the first option is that we need moral strength only when it comes to following already established, morally permissible maxims. The second option, illustrated by Kant's point, implies that moral strength is also needed during the process of maxim adoption. There is some textual evidence in support of the first option, but it has its own pitfalls. I propose a twofold reading according to which Kantian moral strength, conceived as the exercise of our capacity for moral self-control, comes into play not only when it comes to following maxims of virtue but also in the process of their adoption. Moral strength is thus needed for both realizing and setting ourselves moral ends. I turn first to further textual evidence and available interpretations.

## 4.1 Different Interpretations of Moral Strength

Virtue signifies 'a moral strength of the human will [*eine moralische Stärke des Willens*]' (MM 6: 405).[46] It is 'the moral strength of a human being's will in fulfilling his duty' (MM 6: 405), 'the strength of a human being's maxims in fulfilling his duty' (MM 6: 394), and 'the strength of intention [*die Stärke des Vorsatzes*]' (MM 6: 390).[47] Other definitions of virtue, such as 'moral disposition in struggle" (CPrR 5: 84) and moral self-constraint, presuppose the idea that we ought to acquire moral strength.

Some Kant scholars seem to hold that moral strength is not essential to virtue. Robert Johnson and Adam Cureton (2017) argue that one can act from duty while lacking moral strength when one is not tempted to act otherwise. Along these lines, Laura Papish (2007: 141–42) suggests that the moral worth of an action does not depend on moral strength. Although it sounds plausible to say that moral strength is not needed if an agent is already inclined to help, Kant's view seems to be that even this agent must control himself not to perform a morally good action simply from his natural inclination to help. Fulfilling the duty of beneficence requires a proper maxim, and the inclination to help cannot produce such a maxim (CPrR 5: 118). If the agent is to adopt a maxim of virtue, he must acquire inner freedom by setting aside all inclinations and their ends. Otherwise, he will not be in a position to set himself the moral end of increasing others' happiness by adopting a maxim of helping them (MM 6: 452). Hence, I believe that moral strength is needed whenever we are to perform a morally worthy action.[48]

In line with this, Kant points out that moral strength is one aspect of our capacity for self-control: 'For while the capacity (*facultas*) to overcome all

---

[46] Discussions in this section draw on my article on moral strength (Vujošević, 2020a).

[47] See also Anth 7: 147; MM 6: 392, 6: 447; L-Eth 27: 456, 27: 465, 27: 492, 27: 570–1 and 27: 662.

[48] Even if a Kantian moral agent's duty is to refrain from an action, she may still need moral strength for proper maxim adoption. See footnote 16.

sensible impulses can and must be simply *presupposed* in man on account of his freedom, yet this capacity as *strength* (*robur*) is something he must acquire . . .' (MM 6: 397) [italic in the original]. The assumption here is that all of us have an innate capacity for self-control, because 'ought' implies 'can'. We have a duty to acquire moral strength by constantly developing this capacity through its free exercise in accordance with the moral law. Furthermore, 'true strength' of virtue is not only 'a tranquil mind' but also 'a considered and firm resolution to put the law of virtue into practice' (MM 6: 409). Virtue as moral strength is also a kind of self-rule that surpasses the fulfilment of the duty of apathy. This specific aspect of self-control has been read as self-determination. Accordingly, Kant speaks of the moral strength of the human *will* and *maxims*.

Kant's conception of moral strength is sometimes not explained in terms of self-control. Richard McCarty (2009: 196, 230) seems to interpret moral strength as the psychological force of the moral incentive that all of us happen to have. Paul Guyer (2000: 307) argues that virtue in the sense of moral strength is 'caused' by virtue in the sense of a virtuous disposition: moral strength results from an act of inner freedom, which is to be understood as 'an agent's adoption of respect for the moral law as his fundamental maxim'. If I understand it correctly, moral strength is here presented as a causally produced mental state that is not required for acquiring inner freedom.[49]

Anne Margaret Baxley does explain moral strength as the strength of the power of self-control. She states that moral strength is required 'to enforce the morally good choices we legislate to ourselves as autonomous rational agents' (Baxley, 2010: 57). Autocracy is a form of self-control that 'arms us with moral strength to execute self-legislated principles' (Baxley, 2010: 83). This executive power enables compliance with maxims, whereas autonomy is tasked with issuing them.

Jeanine Grenberg (2010) interestingly interprets moral strength as the realization of inner freedom. Vice amounts to 'weak' realizations of inner freedom, which is opposed to 'truer, more complete realizations of inner freedom' (Grenberg, 2010: 163). Whereas the former involves a moment of rationalization, the latter involves keen 'attentiveness' to the moral law by which we fully accept our moral obligations (Grenberg, 2010: 165). Such 'attentiveness' occurs via our moral feeling, and it is by engaging in contemplation of the moral law that we strengthen this feeling. Grenberg seems to hold that this happens before we adopt maxims.

---

[49] If so, maxims of virtue seem to be mere products of already adopted fundamental maxims. For a critique of interpretations that view Kant's notion of *Gesinnung* as a disposition that causally determines our choices, see Julia Peters (2018).

38 *The Philosophy of Immanuel Kant*

I believe that we need to extend the scope of our reading of Kantian moral strength by further explaining the close tie between moral strength and maxim adoption – in conjunction with its connection to Kant's rejection of the model of virtue as a mere habit. In the *Metaphysics of Morals*, Kant objects to defining virtue as 'a long-standing *habit* [*Gewohnheit*] of morally good actions acquired through practice' (6: 383). In the *Anthropology*, he argues against reducing virtue to a 'skill in free lawful actions' (7: 147). But the core of his argument is the same: Were virtue a mere habit, we would have to embrace the unacceptable claim that virtue is a kind of natural mechanism.

In the *Metaphysics of Morals*, Kant therefore emphasizes that virtue can only be a kind of '*free* skill (*habitus libertatis*)' (6: 407) [italic in the original]. It cannot be reduced to consistently acting in accordance with previously established rules but must also involve the free determination of choice in ever-new situations. As Kant explains:

> [M]oral maxims, unlike technical ones, cannot be based on habit [*Gewohnheit*] (since this belongs to the natural constitution of the will's determination); on the contrary, if the practice of virtue were to become a habit the subject would suffer loss to that *freedom* in adopting maxims [*die Freiheit in Nehmung seiner Maximen*] which distinguishes an action done from duty. (MM 6: 409) [italic in the original]

This freedom in adopting maxims is the inner freedom of virtue, and it is why practicing virtue can never become a mere habit.

In line with this, Kant insists that virtue is 'always in progress' (MM 6: 409) and 'can never be completed' (CPrR 5: 33). He suggests that the best we can do is to ensure the 'unending progress' of our *maxims* and 'their constancy in continual progress' (CPrR 5: 32–33). Kant's emphasis on this unending progress may concern the motivating ground of our maxims – which should be constantly renewed – whereas the constancy in this continual progress may concern their purely cognitive, theoretical basis.

In the *Anthropology*, Kant explicitly contrasts virtue as moral strength with skill in performing free lawful actions. He does so by arguing that 'virtue is *moral strength* in fulfilling one's duty, which never should become habit [*Gewohnheit*] but should always emerge entirely new and original from one's way of thinking [*immer ganz neu und ursprünglich aus der Denkungsart hervorgehen soll*]' (Anth 7: 147) [italic in the original]. His point is that virtue as moral strength must always go beyond a mere mechanism of applying certain rules, because the way of thinking characteristic of virtue, or the way of thinking according to moral laws (CPrR 5: 160), can never become habitual or unfree. Moral strength is needed, in ever-new situations, for the process of becoming morally motivated by a proper way of thinking.

# Kant on Self-Control

Without any further explanation of the close link between moral strength and maxim adoption, we risk presupposing a static account of maxims and a mechanistic account of rule application, both of which are ruled out by the above-discussed passages.[50] By making it seem as though moral strength is needed only for following maxims once the activity of adopting them has been completed, we lose a useful tool for accommodating Kant's claim that virtue, as moral strength of the human will, can never become a mere habit. In my view, we can properly capture the freedom in adopting maxims that characterizes maxims of virtue only through providing a proper account of self-control's role in ethical end-setting. Without such an account, we risk underestimating the active and dynamic aspects of Kantian moral strength of will.

What is more, if we were to hold that the strength of intention characteristic of virtue merely concerns an intention to follow established maxims, we would have to say that the fulfilment of duties of virtue merely involves compelling ourselves to perform certain actions. In this way, we would sidestep the very essence of Kantian virtue, which is free self-constraint in end-setting.

## 4.2 The Two Faces of Moral Strength

In his notes to the Doctrine of Virtue (23: 394), Kant writes that moral strength is strength of intention (*Vorsatz*) and strength in action (*That*). By building on this claim, I address two aspects of moral strength. I contend that strength of intention, which is essential to Kantian virtue, cannot be a mere intention to follow our maxims, for it must also be an intention by which we set ourselves moral ends in ever-new situations. This intention is constitutive of maxims of ends, and an end is not simply an action but an aim we intend to realize through the performance (or avoidance) of a particular action. By strength in acting, I mean mere consistency in performing (or avoiding) actions by which we realize moral ends or adhere to our moral maxims.

### 4.2.1 Strength in Realizing Ends

Kant's claims about the strength of our maxims in fulfilling or following our duties (MM 6: 394, 405; Anth 7: 147) support the idea that we need moral strength when it comes to maxim observation. To clarify the role of moral strength in bridging the gap between maxim and deed (Rel 6: 47), I address the notion of cultivation. For Kant, cultivation is an 'active perfecting' of oneself (MM 6: 419). His view is that we can work to ensure to follow our maxims by cultivating our capacities 'for furthering ends set forth by reason'

---

[50] Kant claims that even judging how to apply a maxim 'provides another (subordinate) maxim' (MM 6: 411).

40        *The Philosophy of Immanuel Kant*

(MM 6: 391). Increasing our own natural perfection entails cultivating our natural powers as means for all sorts of possible ends (MM 6: 444). This means that we also cultivate our natural capacities in order to use them as means for realizing those ends that help us to achieve moral ones (MM 6: 392).

In my reading, cultivation involves the proper use of our capacity for self-control. It is the activity of acquiring the strength of self-control by 'abstracting from' sensible impressions, that is, by diverting our attention from them as if they did not exist and, at the same time, becoming conscious of, or attentive to, other representations. To explain why it makes sense to interpret cultivation in this way, I will focus on the cultivation of our capacity for feelings – mainly sympathetic feelings, but also moral feelings.[51] My account of how we cultivate moral feelings highlights the point of intersection of the two faces of moral strength; it enables us to consistently claim that the cultivation of moral feelings can also be involved in the process of adopting virtuous maxims.

Kant argues that we have an indirect duty to cultivate our natural compassionate feelings because this helps us to fulfil our direct duty to 'actively sympathize [*thätige Theilnehmung*]' in the fate of others (MM 6: 457).[52] As he further explains:

> [I]t is therefore an indirect duty to cultivate the compassionate natural (aesthetic) feelings in us, and to make use of them as so many means to sympathy based on moral principles and the feelings appropriate to them. – It is therefore a duty not to avoid the places where the poor who lack the most basic necessities are to be found, but rather to seek them out, and not to shun sickrooms or debtors' prisons and so forth in order to avoid sharing painful feelings one may not be able to resist. (MM 6: 457)

The indirect duty to cultivate our natural receptivity to sharing the feelings of others is usually understood as an intentional self-exposure to scenes of human misery, which is not directly related to self-control.[53] In her excellent discussion of the problem of how to interpret our duty to cultivate our sympathetic feelings so that it fits with Kant's rigid stance on impurity, Marcia Baron (1995: 217) argues that cultivation, conceived as 'seeking out situations that will elicit' compassionate feelings, presupposes the activity of controlling feelings. Her point is that cultivating feelings that are already under our control can make us more sensitive to situations where our help is needed.

---

[51] According to Krista Karbowski Thomason (2017), Kant held that we should not cultivate feelings. Feelings of envy, for example, should indeed not be cultivated. However, Kant claims that sympathetic feelings and moral feelings should be cultivated.

[52] I agree with Wood (2008: 176–77) that the duty of active 'sympathetic participation' involves 'taking part in the life of another'. See also Melissa Seymour Fahmy (2009).

[53] See, for instance, Paul Guyer (2010: 146–47), Nancy Sherman (1990: 158–59) and Randy Cagle (2005: 458).

## Kant on Self-Control 41

In my view, the cultivation of our natural compassionate feelings must involve more than merely exposing ourselves to situations in which our natural compassionate feelings are likely to be intensified. It must also involve the activity of controlling 'our sensitive intake' in such situations. For Kant, the duty to cultivate our natural compassionate feelings cannot simply be a duty to passively share in the suffering of others (Anth 7: 236). If I cannot alleviate someone's suffering, then I should not let myself 'be infected by his pain (through my imagination)', for in doing so I would just increase the amount of suffering in the world (MM 6: 457).[54] Still, the duty to cultivate our compassionate feelings requires not that we become indifferent to all suffering but that we strengthen these feelings so that they cannot affect us against our will. Unlike the weakness of sentimentality (*Empfindelei*), sensitivity (*Empfindsamkeit*) 'is a capacity [*Vermögen*] and a strength [*Stärke*], which either permits or prevents the states of both pleasure and displeasure from entering the mind' (Anth 7: 236; translation modified).

Were we, as Baron (1995: 220) suggests, to cultivate just those feelings that are already under our control, we would be cultivating not our natural feelings but their refined versions. Cultivation is better understood as the activity of acquiring the strength of moral self-control by 'abstracting from' certain sensible impressions. When cultivating our natural compassionate feelings, we exercise our capacity for self-control not simply by compelling ourselves to visit places of human misery but also by controlling the state of representations in our minds. Visiting such places puts us in situations where we can best fulfil our indirect duty to cultivate our compassionate feelings, which makes it possible to fulfil our direct duty to 'actively sympathize' with the fate of others. At the same time, we develop our capacity for self-control by setting aside forceful sensible impressions, such as the sight of someone in great pain. As Kant explains, the faculty of abstraction is 'a strength of mind that can only be acquired through practice' (Anth 7: 132).[55]

Cultivating our natural compassionate feelings by exposing ourselves to scenes of human misery requires that we control these feelings so that they do not become affects. We ought to control our natural sympathetic feelings by disregarding the sensible impressions that would otherwise make them so

---

[54] We suffer with others by means of the power of imagination (Anth 7: 238–9), and we can also strengthen our natural sympathetic feelings by gaining control over our sympathetic power of imagination (Anth 7: 179, 203).

[55] Since such cultivation of our powers helps us to fulfil our duties to others, visiting places of human misery does not seem to amount to using others merely as means.

42 *The Philosophy of Immanuel Kant*

intense as to overwhelm us. Unlike affects, sympathetic feelings that are under our control can help us to realize moral ends.[56]

But the final aim of the cultivation of our natural sympathetic feelings is their refinement into moral sympathetic feelings – the feelings of which we become conscious in a new light once we have decided to act as the moral law demands. By setting aside our natural sympathetic feelings in the process of adopting moral maxims, we facilitate the adoption of maxims of virtue, which makes us aware of these feelings as being based on moral principles.[57] These cultivated feelings are constitutive of the virtue of 'active' sympathy or our active concern for the well-being of others.

The activities by which we cultivate our feelings may also be directly involved in the process of adopting moral maxims on which we really act. If we take a step further by setting aside all inclinations and the feelings on which they are based, we then also cultivate or strengthen our moral feelings. Through this abstracting activity all feelings arising from sensible impressions lose their influence, and moral feeling becomes more powerful (MM 6: 408). The cultivation of our natural susceptibility to moral feeling might be understood as an aspect of acquiring control over the condition of certain representations in our minds. In the calm state of mind into which we enter by fulfilling the duty of apathy, moral feeling, as the genuine moral motive, gains its full motivational strength and enables us to adopt virtuous maxims of ends.

### 4.2.2 Strength in Setting Ends

Were we to reduce the specifically virtuous intention to a firm intention to consistently perform actions in accordance with our fully established maxims, we would have to presuppose that we have a prepared set of maxims, some of which we 'take off the shelf' simply as they are and apply to real-life situations. But as we have seen, this is not how Kant understands virtuous maxims and their adoption. The strength of intention that Kant calls virtue (MM 6: 390) cannot simply be the strength of intention to perform certain actions but must also be the strength of an intention by which we, in ever-new situations, set ourselves particular moral ends that motivate us to perform morally good actions. Insofar

---

[56] The cultivation of our natural sympathetic feelings can actually serve as a 'means to sympathy based on moral principles and the feelings appropriate to them' (MM 6: 457) in two senses. It can be a means of facilitating both the observation and the adoption of virtuous maxims. The latter usually escapes scholarly notice. On my account, cultivated sympathetic feelings also enable proper maxim adoption by facilitating free reflection.

[57] Kant speaks of cultivation in terms of attentiveness (e.g. MM 6: 401) and explains abstraction as a specific way of becoming conscious of certain representations (Anth 7: 131).

## Kant on Self-Control

as maxims of virtue are to guide our actions in practice, they must involve this kind of intention.

By 'strength of soul [*Stärke der Seele*]' Kant means 'strength of intention [*Stärke des Vorsatzes*] in a human being as a being endowed with freedom, hence his strength insofar as he is in control of himself . . . and so in the state of health proper to a human being' (MM 6: 384). This strength involves the elementary form of self-control required for maintaining sound mental health. But Kant here primarily seems to have in mind the strength of a pure moral intention, for he continues by arguing that it is improper to ask whether great crimes require more strength of soul than virtues (MM 6: 384).

In the *Groundwork* (4: 398), Kant connects moral strength with maxims by pointing to the moral content of maxims: '[I]f an unfortunate man, strong of soul [*stark an Seele*] . . . wishes for death and yet preserves his life without loving it, not from inclination or fear, but from duty, then his maxim has moral content [*moralischen Gehalt*]'. Despite his powerful aversion to life, this man shows moral strength by deciding to preserve his life, motivated by the representation of duty. His maxim therefore has moral content. Kant's point seems to be that even someone who loves life needs moral strength to adopt a virtuous maxim, because his immediate inclination toward life cannot stand for the pure moral content of his maxim. If we are to become morally motivated, we should abstract from all impure incentives so that we can subordinate the incentives of our inclinations to the incentive of the moral law. Moral strength is necessary for the adoption of maxims of virtue – maxims with a pure incentive that is sufficiently strong to determine one's choice to perform an action (MM 6: 480).

Given Kant's overall emphasis on the form of maxims and the universalization test, discussions regarding the content or subjective motivating ground of our maxims may appear irrelevant. Nevertheless, Kant claims neither that our maxims lack content nor that their content is irrelevant. He argues that incentives are the matter of our maxims (Rel 6: 36), that the matter (the end) should be conditioned by the form (the law) (MM 6: 376–7), and that every maxim of action 'contains an end [*Zweck*]' (MM 6: 395; G 4: 436). There 'can be no will' without some end (TP 8: 279) and a morally worthy action implies taking an interest in an end. Intending a particular moral end requires making a continuous effort to put aside inclinations or to purify our incentives in new situations; that is, it requires that we acquire moral strength by properly exercising our capacity for self-control in ever-new situations, so as to avoid adopting maxims for the sake of the ends of inclinations.

Moral strength is then required if we are to secure the purity of the subjective motivating ground of our maxims of virtue in new situations. We seem to make the categorical imperative subjectively necessary by setting ourselves particular

44 *The Philosophy of Immanuel Kant*

moral ends, or by actually determining our choices by the pure moral incentive. Moral strength is needed for us to incorporate the moral law into our maxims as a pure incentive that actually moves us to perform a certain action, and this must be done in a given situation.

My point is not that we need completely new, differently formulated maxims all the time. I am merely claiming that their subjective, motivating ground must be renewed in different situations and that moral strength is necessary for this renewing, purifying activity. Moral agents of all stripes can check in advance whether a maxim would qualify as a universal law. This purely cognitive, theoretical basis of our maxims makes an action 'objectively necessary' (MM 6: 218) and does not depend on our constantly acquiring moral strength by properly exercising our capacity for self-control.

Kant explains how we acquire moral strength by suggesting that our innate capacity for self-control can be called a 'strength' if we think of it as not simply given:

> [T]his capacity as *strength* (*robur*) is something he must acquire through [a process in which] by contemplation [*Betrachtung*] (*contemplatione*) of the dignity of the pure moral law in us, the moral *incentive* (the thought of the law) is elevated [*erhoben*], but at the same time also through *exercise* [*zugleich aber auch durch Übung*] (*exercitio*). (MM 6: 397; translation modified) [italic in the original]

We acquire moral strength through contemplation of the dignity of the moral law, but at the same time through the exercise of our capacity for self-control. This is where my interpretation departs from Grenberg's valuable account. In my reading, contemplation does not suffice. Our way of acquiring moral strength cannot be reduced to mere awareness of the categorical nature of the moral law, and the realization of inner freedom must involve more. If it is to suffice as a characterization of Kantian moral strength, Grenberg's 'keen attentiveness' to the moral law must be conceived as an activity with a more dynamic and active aspect – it must go hand in hand with the activity of developing our capacity for self-control over time and incorporating 'the law in its purity' into our maxims (MM 6: 217).[58] By properly incorporating the incentive of the moral law into our maxims, or by freely adopting our maxims of virtue, we make the moral law a self-sufficient moral incentive that actually moves us to perform a certain action. Via self-control, we divert our attention away from our inclinations and focus on the moral ends that maxims of virtue must contain.

---

[58] If so, we can deal with certain responsibility issues without appealing to Grenberg's (2010: 163) distinction between 'weak' and 'truer' realizations of inner freedom.

If so, we acquire moral strength through self-constraint – via moral feeling – only if this happens through the adoption of our virtuous maxims. Grenberg's suggestion seems to be that we cultivate our moral feelings simply by engaging in contemplation, that is, merely by becoming aware of the demands of the moral law. On my account, we must take a step further when cultivating our moral feelings. A person who fails to cultivate moral feeling remains unaffected by the concepts of duty. Our own concept of duty is 'constraint [*Nöthigung*] to an end adopted reluctantly', and it is through moral feeling that 'one makes one's object every particular end that is also a duty' (MM 6: 386–87). By cultivating moral feelings, we constrain ourselves to adopt moral ends or accept that the constraint present in the concept of duty really holds for us. We do so by adopting maxims of virtue. As elaborated, moral feeling plays a crucial role in the adoption of the subjective principles through which we actually determine our choices.

Importantly, Kant also suggests that moral feeling is the pure virtuous disposition (MM 6: 387). In his view, the purest virtuous disposition is 'inner morally practical perfection' and moral perfection 'consists subjectively in the purity (*puritas moralis*) of one's disposition to duty, namely in the law being itself alone the incentive, even without the admixture of aims derived from sensibility' (MM 6: 387; 6: 446). The end of moral perfection, as one of the ends that we ought to set to ourselves, consists in purity of moral disposition. By setting ourselves a pure virtuous disposition as an end, we intend to determine our choice by the thought of the moral law alone.

Moral feeling is the subjective motivating ground of our maxims, which we cultivate through adopting maxims of virtue. It is through the activity of acquiring moral strength that we acquire a virtuous disposition or moral perfection. Kant claims that the duty to increase one's own moral perfection includes 'the cultivation of one's will (moral way of thinking) [*seines Willens (sittlicher Denkungsart)*]' and that a person has a duty to carry the cultivation of his *will* 'up to the purest virtuous disposition, in which the *law* becomes also the incentive to his actions that conform with duty and he obeys the law from duty' (MM 6: 387, translation modified) [italic in the original]. Acquiring a virtuous disposition therefore consists in cultivating our will (or our moral way of thinking) by adopting maxims in which the pure moral law becomes an incentive that actually moves us to act.

A moral intention, then, must be an intention by which we set the end of moral perfection, and we strengthen this intention by abstracting from sensible impressions. The strength of intention that Kant calls virtue seems to consist in sticking to our general commitment to the moral law by constantly renewing our more general moral intention (*Absicht*) in new situations.

46 *The Philosophy of Immanuel Kant*

In conclusion, the above analysis of moral strength as a proper exercise of our capacity for self-control has shown that Kantian moral strength is necessary not only for compelling ourselves to realize moral ends but also for setting ourselves those ends in the process of maxim adoption. Accordingly, the intention the strength of which is constitutive of virtue must also be the intention by which we set ourselves particular moral ends. We acquire this strength of intention by exercising our capacity for abstraction in ever-new situations. Without moral strength, our maxims would not be the principles that actually guide our actions in practice. This reading captures the active and dynamic aspect of Kantian moral strength. It explains why Kant speaks of the moral strength of the human will and maxims, and it accommodates Kant's insistence that virtue can never become a mere habit.

## 5 Moral Weakness: The Other Side of the Coin

Drawing on the previous section, I will interpret Kant's conception of moral weakness as a mere lack of the strength necessary for setting ourselves particular moral ends and realizing them. In my view, moral weakness is expressed at both intimately related levels of self-control. My aim is to propose a reading that consistently unifies Kant's suggestions that moral weakness is a failure to follow maxims and a manifestation of the first grade of our propensity to evil. In order to account for the latter suggestion, I will try to describe what precisely goes wrong at the level of maxim adoption when it comes to the morally weak agent. Before presenting my account, I will sketch the puzzle of how to understand the weakness of will in Kant's theoretical framework and evaluate a selection of available solutions.

### 5.1 The Puzzle of Weakness of Will

At first glance, weakness of will might seem easy to explain. It is acting against our better judgement. But how weakness of will is possible is a matter of debate.[59] Consider the one who judges that he should stop smoking for the sake of his health but still lights up another cigarette. There is a principle that he holds dear, and there is his failure to act accordingly. The problem arises when it comes to explaining this failure such that weakness of will involves *freely* acting against one's better judgement. If the agent's smoking another cigarette is explained by his being overpowered by an irresistible desire to smoke – such that he could not do otherwise – this would seem to be a case of compulsion. And if the agent decides to smoke the cigarette, or forms an intention to do so,

---

[59] See, for instance, Donald Davidson (1980) [1969], Gary Watson (1977) and Alfred Mele (1987).

we might think that he has changed his mind, but then the conflict that is essential to weakness of will disappears. The further question is how this decision, or intention, is related to his better judgement. Perhaps he has decided to smoke just this last cigarette because he is nervous and believes that smoking will calm him. Deep down, he may still hold that he should stop smoking for health reasons, but he now has one more, conflicting reason. One may be tempted to say that the solution is simply that his strongest reason or desire wins, but this simple answer pushes us back to the problem of how to explain freely acting against one's better judgement.

Situating Kant's brief treatment of moral weakness within his own ethical framework complicates the issue even further.[60] On the one hand, Kant suggests that moral weakness is a mere failure to follow our otherwise morally good maxims. He mentions the 'weakness of the human heart in complying with the adopted maxims' (Rel 6: 29) and argues that the weak are not 'strong enough to comply with' their 'adopted principles' (Rel 6: 37).[61] This easily leads to the conclusion that moral weakness is merely expressed at the level of following maxims. On the other hand, Kant addresses moral weakness as the first grade of our propensity to evil, which implies that moral weakness must also be expressed at the level of maxim adoption. This propensity 'must reside in the subjective ground of the possibility of the deviation of the maxims from the moral law' (Rel 6: 29), and it is 'the subjective universal ground of the adoption of a transgression into our maxim' (Rel 6: 41). It is still ambiguous whether, and if so how, these two aspects of moral weakness can be combined.

Furthermore, it has been argued that what we usually call weakness of will is incompatible with Henry Allison's incorporation thesis, which is his interpretation of Kant's passage on what characterizes freedom of the power of choice (Rel 6: 24). Allison (1990: 40) claims that 'an inclination or desire does not of itself constitute a reason for acting'; it becomes such a reason only when we incorporate it into one of our maxims.[62] The general concern is that Allison's

---

[60] This section is based on Vujošević (2019).

[61] Although Kant sometimes uses the terms 'weakness of heart' and 'frailty' interchangeably, he also seems to make the following subtle distinction: the weak heart is the manifestation of frailty, which is the first grade of the propensity to evil. He suggests that the quality of one's heart arises from this propensity (Rel 6: 29). My aim is not to try to explain the origin of frailty but to describe how it manifests itself in new situations as weakness of heart.

[62] Jens Timmermann (2022: 97) criticizes this interpretative move by claiming that no textual evidence supports the intellectualist reading according to which the incorporation of an incentive into a maxim consists in taking it to be a reason. Timmermann (2022: 108) argues that incorporation is the task of the faculty of choice, which 'itself has nothing to do with judgement'. The gap between judgement and choice is meant to explain weakness of will. Kant indeed suggests that the incorporation of incentives into maxims is the act of choice. But what I find less convincing are the claims that choosing our maxims has nothing to do with judgement and that the cognitive can be so strictly separated from the motivational. I believe that Kant's conception

# 48    *The Philosophy of Immanuel Kant*

incorporation thesis makes acting against one's better judgement impossible: moral weakness, as a failure to act in accordance with an adopted maxim, would then be based on yet another maxim, which again presupposes the incorporation of incentives.[63]

On the other hand, the claim that Kant's notion of weakness is not expressed at the level of the incorporation of incentives falls prey to the difficulty of how to account for moral weakness as freely acting against one's better judgement and as a manifestation of our propensity to evil. The morally weak agent does incorporate the law into his maxim, although not in a fully satisfying way (Rel 6: 29). If so, then we need an account of what goes wrong when it comes to the weak-willed person's incorporation of incentives into her maxims.

There is an additional problem of how to distinguish between the weak, the impure, the vicious and the virtuous, especially with regard to how they incorporate incentives into their maxims. Impurity (*Unlauterkeit*) is the second stage of our propensity to evil, which leads to actions that are not done 'purely from duty' (Rel 6: 30). Viciousness (*Bösartigkeit*) is the third and worst grade of evil, which involves the subordination of the incentive of the moral law to the incentives of inclinations (Rel 6: 30). Unlike the vicious agent, the weak agent does not incorporate deviation from the moral law into her maxims by allowing the incentives of inclination to determine her choice, but it is less clear how she differs from the impure agent and the virtuous agent.

Kant scholars have come up with a variety of creative solutions to the outlined problems. Some employ a conceptual distinction between motivating and justifying reasons. David Sussman (2001) uses Kant's treatment of the passions to account for weakness, whereas Patrick Frierson (2014) argues that weakness is a defect of volition that is opposed to passions. However, very few of the available solutions are based on Kant's notion of the moral strength that is constitutive of virtue. This is surprising, especially because Kant explains moral weakness as a mere lack of moral strength (MM 6: 384, 6: 390).

## 5.2 A Look at Paradigmatic Solutions

The widespread assumption is that Kantian moral weakness can only be exhibited at the level of following morally good maxims. Stephen Engstrom (1988: 441) holds that 'the frail agent's weakness is not expressed in any maxim', and Maria Borges (2019: 24) claims that weakness 'is an exception not reflected in the maxim'. Richard McCarty (1993) argues that Kant's treatment of weakness

---

of moral weakness can be properly explained only if we leave room for weakness at the level of judgement and maxim adoption.

[63] See Marcia Baron (1993) and Robert Johnson (1998).

enables us to accommodate those cases in which we have a genuinely moral maxim but fail to live up to it. His point is that the weak-willed agent recognizes the moral law as providing a sufficient reason but fails to act morally because his moral feelings do not happen to be sufficiently strong.

However, this need not exhaust the scope of Kantian moral weakness. The fact that Kant addresses weakness as the first stage of our propensity to evil speaks against the idea that there is nothing wrong with the maxims of the morally weak. Kant emphasizes that evil must not be sought in inclinations, but in one's 'perverted maxims': 'genuine evil consists in our *will* not to resist the inclinations' (Rel 6: 58–9). Moreover, Kantian moral weakness cannot be explained in terms of the strength of the incentives that we happen to have. As 'the impotence of the incentive of reason' (Rel 6: 59), moral weakness must also be explained as the weakness of the human *will* in facing temptations.

Some insightful interpretations leave room for weakness at the level of maxim adoption. The inner conflict experienced by the morally weak agent is conceived as a conflict between his good underlying maxim and his morally incorrect particular maxim. Thomas Hill (2012: 146) argues that the morally weak agent 'must be viewed as having two conflicting maxims: a basic maxim to conform to morality's unconditional requirements and a shorter-term maxim reflecting an intention to indulge self-love on the particular occasion'. Robert Johnson similarly argues that the Kantian weak-willed agent's disposition or underlying maxim is morally good, whereas his specific maxims are not: just like the vicious agent, he incorporates 'wayward incentives' into his 'motives' (Johnson, 1998: 362). Both have and follow morally incorrect particular maxims. When making a snide comment to a colleague, the weak and the vicious are therefore both 'motivated by a maxim of doing so' (Johnson, 1998: 361–62). The only difference is that the weak agent acts against his own deepest commitments, because he does not have an evil disposition.

First, this kind of philosophically appealing solution seems to work only on the assumption that the morally weak agent's underlying maxim or disposition is genuinely good. But as I will explain, this presupposition can be challenged by textual evidence. Second, the above-described way of accounting for the inner conflict experienced by the morally weak agent seems to rest on a very sharp distinction between particular and underlying maxims. The latter are thought to be static, for they are meant to represent our deepest commitments, which are made once and for all, independently of our particular maxims. The implication of this view seems to be that one who often adopts and follows specific immoral maxims, might still be said to have a good underlying maxim. Hence, even someone who often intentionally reverses the ethical order of the incentives in his particular maxims, might still be said to have a good

50 *The Philosophy of Immanuel Kant*

subjective, motivating ground of his particular maxims. Third, as I elaborate below, the claim that the weak person adopts the same particular maxims as the vicious person falls prey to the difficulty of explaining why Kant highlights that vice, unlike weakness, is an 'intentional [*vorsetzliche*]' transgression that 'has become a principle' (MM 6: 390). If understood as an intentional transgression of the moral law based on a maxim, making a snide comment to a colleague would seem to illustrate the Kantian vice of arrogance rather than weakness. Finally, even if we could distinguish between the vicious and the weak in terms of their different underlying maxims, this would leave no room for the impure. To the extent that the impure agent has a morally good disposition, his failure is conflated with weakness, and to the extent that his disposition is evil, it is conflated with vice.

Mark Timmons (1994) interestingly applies the distinction between motivating and justifying reasons by arguing that the morally weak person still has an evil disposition. He leaves room for moral weakness at the level of adopting maxims, but his explanation depends on the idea of moral luck. The question is whether such an explanation can accommodate the freedom condition of weakness of will and other responsibility-related issues. Adopting maxims and acting accordingly should not be a matter of luck on a Kantian picture. As Kant suggests, this is better spelled out in terms of self-control, or the lack thereof. In what follows, I examine moral weakness as a failure to properly exercise our capacity for self-control when setting ourselves particular moral ends and realizing them.[64] This examination will help us to understand what is going wrong at the level of maxim adoption when it comes to the morally weak.

## 5.3 A Self-Control-Based Solution

Weakness is a 'mere lack of virtue [*blos Untugend*]', or a mere 'lack of moral strength (*defectus moralis*)' (MM 6: 390; 6: 384). It is possible to lack virtue as moral strength in two ways. One can exhibit either a 'negative lack of virtue' or a lack of virtue that is also positive (MM 6: 384). The former is weakness and the latter is vice. If virtue is '+a', then weakness is '0' and vice is '−a' (MM 6: 384 and Rel 6: 22 n).

Vice is an intentional transgression of the moral law based on a morally incorrect maxim, in which one consciously reverses the ethical order of the incentives. The vicious agent is aware of the moral law, but she does not properly incorporate it into her maxims. When adopting her maxims, she starts

---

[64] In his inspiring account, Hill (2012) approaches moral weakness as lack of moral strength, although not primarily in relation to setting moral ends and self-determination. As explained in section 5.2, there is also an important aspect of his interpretation that I am unwilling to accept.

## Kant on Self-Control 51

from the ends that she is anyway eager to adopt and does not constrain herself to adopt moral ends. Just like Kant's moral egoist, the vicious person 'puts the supreme determining ground of his will simply in utility and happiness, not in the thought of duty' (Anth 7: 130).[65]

By claiming that the weak agent adopts the same maxims as the vicious agent, we are then conflating a merely negative lack of virtue with a lack of virtue that is also positive. The morally weak agent does not yet seem to locate the determining ground of her will in one of her self-seeking interests. She does not yet seem to adopt maxims on empirical grounds by intentionally reversing the ethical order of her incentives. The maxim that guided Sulla in his bloody revenge against his enemies cannot be attributed to the weak agent. The latter is someone who is willing to help others but fails to do so.

This easily leads to the conclusion that the weak agent has the same particular maxims as the virtuous agent but simply fails to perform certain actions. But if so, it becomes difficult to explain why Kant treats weakness as the first stage of evil. In an attempt to solve this problem, we can best analyse weakness as a lack of moral strength of the human *will* and *maxims* (MM 6: 447, 6: 394, 6: 405). For example, the duty of beneficence 'consists in the subject's being constrained by his reason to adopt this maxim as a universal law' (MM 6: 452); it does not require that the agent performs the action of helping whenever he sees someone in need. On its own, the mere omission of an action can hardly count as a lack of Kantian virtue. I believe that Kantian moral weakness is best understood as a mere lack of moral strength that plays out on two levels. After briefly clarifying the weak-willed agent's lack of self-control as a mere failure to adhere to his maxims, I try to describe his lack of self-control at the level of maxim adoption.

Kant describes weakness as follows:

> First, the frailty (*fragilitas*) of human nature is expressed even in the complaint of an Apostle: 'I have the will, but the execution is lacking [*Wollen habe ich wohl, aber das Vollbringen fehlt*]' i.e. I incorporate the good (the law) into the maxim of my power of choice; but this good which is an irresistible incentive objectively or ideally (*in thesi*), is subjectively (*in hypothesi*) the weaker (in comparison with inclination) whenever the maxim is to be followed. (Rel 6: 29; translation modified)

This passage makes clear that Kantian moral weakness is a lack of moral strength in compelling oneself to realize moral ends. Kant also mentions 'the general weakness [*Schwäche*] of the human heart in complying with the adopted

---

[65] He can be said to have 'no touchstone at all of the genuine concept of duty' (Anth 7: 130). For Kant, adopting maxims on empirical grounds yields no concept of duty (MM 6: 382).

52       *The Philosophy of Immanuel Kant*

maxims anyway [*überhaupt*]' (Rel 6: 29; translation modified). The weak agent may lack the skill to compel himself to act a certain way. He might lack the self-discipline necessary to obey rules or fail to acquire a habit of acting a certain way.

The weak agent may also fail to follow his maxims because he has failed to cultivate his capacities in order to use them as means to realize all kinds of ends. For example, by exercising one's capacity for judging in different situations one becomes more skilful in fulfilling the duties of virtue. The skill of postponing judgement, developed through practice, 'indicates great strength of mind' by which we can avoid performing bad actions out of anger (L-Eth 27: 365).[66]

The weak agent might also be under the sway of an affect and therefore momentarily incapable of acting in accordance with his maxims. Kant claims that 'weakness in the use of one's understanding coupled with the strength of one's emotions' is 'only a lack of virtue [*Untugend*]' (MM 6: 408). A lack of moral strength due to affects can be an aspect of Kant's conception of moral weakness. The weak agent might fail to cultivate his capacity for self-control and therefore descend into affective states that make him momentarily incapable of controlling himself and adhering to his maxims. Furthermore, by allowing his feelings to become affects, he also creates the obstacles that stand in the way of self-determination and proper maxim adoption. And yet, if understood simply as lack of moral strength due to affects, lack of virtue cannot provide a full account of Kantian moral weakness. We also need to address lack of moral strength in setting aside those feelings on which inclinations are based. In this way, one cultivates or strengthens one's susceptibility to moral feelings. As elaborated in the previous two sections, this cultivation enables the adoption of maxims of virtue.

A fuller application of what has been said about the connection between moral feeling and moral strength provides us with a plausible portrait of the morally weak agent. If the weak agent fails to cultivate moral feeling and if it is by strengthening our moral feeling that we make our object every particular end that is a duty (MM 6: 387), then the weak agent fails to intend a particular moral end. She takes no interest in particular moral ends because she has failed to cultivate her capacity for moral feeling, conceived as the capacity to take a pure interest (CPrR 5: 79–80). For this reason, she remains unaffected by the concepts of duty. Her general, abstract knowledge of what is morally right or wrong does not effectively motivate her. By failing to cultivate one of the natural predispositions of the mind to being affected by the concepts of duty (MM 6: 399), or the subjective ground on which she is morally to determine her choices, she fails to enter into a state in which

---

[66] This ability to defer judgements is a major element of autocracy (L-Eth 27: 366).

the moral law actually determines her power of choice. Her *maxims* remain *weak* or impotent in practice.

Finally, Kant also implies that moral feeling is the purest virtuous disposition and that this disposition, conceived as the end of moral perfection, can be attained by cultivating the will or our 'moral way of thinking' (MM 6: 387).[67] If so, then the weak agent may fail to achieve this disposition because she fails to cultivate her moral way of thinking by adopting maxims of virtue – the subjective principles of actions through which we actually determine our choices. Since she fails to cultivate her natural capacity for moral feeling, she can be said to set herself the end of moral perfection, but only in the sense of having an overly general, wishful intention to cultivate her will. Her commitment to the moral law remains a wishful moral intention, because she fails to strengthen or renew this general intention by continually exercising her capacity for self-control in order to abstract from sensible impressions. She fails to acquire the strength of the intention that is constitutive of maxims of virtue or maxims of ends.

This puts us in a better position to answer the question of whether the weak agent's disposition, or her fundamental maxim, is a genuinely good one. I agree with Johnson and Hill that the morally weak agent has a kind of general, pure commitment to do what is right. Unlike the vicious agent, the weak agent can be said to have a general intention to do what the moral law demands. The weak agent wants to do what she ought to do (Rel 6: 29). She can be said to set herself moral ends in a purely intellectual and abstract way. The objective determining ground of her choice might be characterized as good. As Kant explains, the weak agent incorporates the moral law as the good that is 'an irresistible incentive objectively' (Rel 6: 29). However, I do not think that this explanation suffices to show that the disposition of the morally weak agent is genuinely good, because her abstractly good commitment to the moral law remains fragile in practice. The Kantian weak-willed agent might take mere wishes, which 'always remain empty of deeds, for proof of a good heart' (MM 6: 441). She might deceive herself into thinking that she cannot compel herself to act morally in some situations.[68] Since

---

[67] He also suggests that moral feeling is our original predisposition (*Anlage*) to the good (Rel 6: 27–8) and that this predisposition gradually becomes a way of thinking by which the moral law becomes a self-sufficient incentive (Rel 6: 48).

[68] My reading can include self-deception without claiming that the weak agent is by definition unaware of what she ought to do. Her overly general intention to act morally is not powerful enough in practice because she fails to exercise her capacity for self-control. There is disagreement in the literature concerning whether self-deception is a necessary condition of an evil disposition. Addressing this question would go beyond the scope of this Element. An overview of the different positions and the argument that self-deceptive rationalization necessarily conditions evil can be found in Laura Papish (2018). Papish (2018: 100–01) conceptualizes self-deceptive rationalization as 'a truth-preserving pattern of distraction', which she explains in terms of refocusing attention on one's own unhappiness. As explained earlier, Kantian distraction is more a dispersion of one's

54 *The Philosophy of Immanuel Kant*

there is no middle position between good and evil for Kant (Rel 6: 24; 6: 22 n), we must conclude that the weak agent's disposition is evil.

We may also resist the conclusion that the disposition of the morally weak agent is genuinely good by appealing to Kant's sophisticated version of the criterion for distinguishing moral good from evil – we incorporate both the incentive of the moral law and the incentives of inclination, so that the difference between good and evil must lie in the way they are incorporated (Rel 6: 36). The suggestion is that being morally good means that one has incorporated the law into one's fundamental maxim (*oberste Maxime*) as a by-itself-sufficient (*für sich allein hinreichend*) determination of one's choice (Rel 6: 36). The weak agent might then incorporate the incentive of the moral law but fail to incorporate it as a self-sufficient incentive.

The impure agent can be said to do the same, however. Kant points out that his maxims are 'not purely moral' (Rel 6: 30). The impure agent intends to comply with the law from morally unacceptable motives, and the weak agent wishes to comply with the law from morally acceptable motives. There is also a further difference with regard to the quality of their maxims. The maxims of the impure agent can be 'powerful enough in practice' (Rel 6: 30) in that they result in legally good actions, whereas the maxims of the weak agent are not effective in practice. So, although the weak and the impure can both be said to incorporate the incentive of the moral law improperly, they seem to do so for different reasons and in slightly different ways. The subjective motivating ground of the maxims of the weak agent is pure, but his pure intention to follow the law is ultimately impotent in practice because he seems to postpone the adoption of particular moral maxims that are efficient in practice. The weak agent does not seem to adopt impure maxims based on the incentives of inclination, but he fails to renew his general commitment to the moral law by reassessing his incentives in new situations. The impure agent seems to take a step further to the extent that he adopts impure maxims in which priority is more explicitly given to morally unacceptable incentives to follow the moral law.

We can clarify what goes wrong at the level of maxim adoption when it comes to the morally weak by recalling Kant's claim that all lawgiving consists of two elements: a law, which represents an action as objectively necessary, and an incentive, which makes that action also subjectively necessary (MM 6: 218). The first element suffices for a possible determination of choice, and the second is required for actual self-determination (MM 6: 218). Accordingly, even

---

attention than a refocusing on something else. But I agree with the idea that distraction can be involved in self-deception.

though the purely theoretical basis of the morally weak agent's maxims is good, there may still be something wrong with the subjective, motivating ground of his maxims, which is what enables actual self-determination. Something may still not be totally right with the content or ends of his maxims. The maxims of the weak agent seem to lack a proper element that would make them, as Kant puts it, 'subjectively practical' (L-Met 28: 317) or 'subjectively possible' (L-Met 29: 900). Objectively, as regards the rule, his maxims are good, but subjectively, as regards the incentive, they are not (Rel 6: 58 n). The incentive of the moral law may be irresistible ideally – '*in thesi*', but not also '*in hypothesi*' (Rel 6: 29). In the human condition, the subjective ground of its irresistibility may be weaker than the inclinations. One can will the good but not strongly enough to move one to perform a morally right action. It is through the constant exercise of our capacity for moral self-control that our maxims become strong enough to result in actions, for this is how we set ourselves particular moral ends.[69]

The maxims of the morally weak agent may thus be more like practical laws, which would serve him 'subjectively as the practical principles' of his action if his reason were to *gain control* over his faculty of desire (G 4: 401 n). Since he does not properly exercise his capacity for self-control, his self-imposed rules do not function as volitional principles that actually motivate him to act morally. His maxims are not strong enough to actually move him to act. This may also be why the weak agent is not 'strong enough to comply with' his 'adopted principles [*genommenen Grundsätze*]' (Rel 6: 37).

As I have shown, it is through the constant exercise of our capacity for moral self-control, or through the acquisition of moral strength, that our maxims become the principles that actually guide our actions in practice. It is only via a constant effort to set aside the influence of sensible impressions on our mind that we can set ourselves moral ends in new situations. My point has been that the intention the strength of which Kant calls virtue (MM 6: 390) is an intention by which we set ourselves particular moral ends and that our particular maxims must include this intention if we are to be motivated by the pure moral incentive to perform an action. Without such an intention, our maxims would not be subjectively practical principles of our own volition.

On the basis of these considerations, I now conclude that the morally weak agent lacks virtue, understood as acquired moral strength. He lacks the strength of intention needed to set himself moral ends in ever-new situations. For this reason, the weak agent's maxims do not seem to be subjectively practical. The

---

[69] Recall that Kant himself speaks of the strength of maxims (MM 6: 394, 6: 447; Rel 6: 48 and NMM 23: 396).

56 *The Philosophy of Immanuel Kant*

agent who does not acquire moral strength by properly exercising his capacity for self-control is weak. He fails to make a continuous effort to sustain the firmness of his general moral intention in the face of contrary inclinations. The subjective determining ground of his choice remains impotent in practice, because he fails to continuously use his capacity for self-control to put aside the incentives of inclinations. By failing to gradually acquire virtue, he fails to restore his original predisposition to the good. This reading is in agreement with Kant's point that from our own perspective, the reformation of our propensity to evil as a perverted way of thinking (*verkehrter Denkungsart*) must be gradual because we can judge the *strength* of our maxims only on the basis of the control over the input of sensibility that we gain over time (Rel 6: 48).

The weak agent may not be strong enough to comply with the principles that he endorses on a purely theoretical level because he seems to postpone making these principles subjectively practical. For example, although he generally holds that he should help those in need and makes the happiness of others his end *in abstracto*, this does not sufficiently motivate him to help others. The rule 'help others in need' does not become a subjectively practical principle that moves him to perform the relevant actions.

Once he succumbs to the temptation to adopt impure maxims, he becomes not only weak but also impure. To use the same example, he adopts the maxims that often result in acts of helping others, but he does not do so 'from duty'. But even if the weak agent does not become impure, his way of thinking cannot rightly be characterized as virtuous, because he fails to carry out his overly general commitment to the law in practice. He fails to continuously renew his commitment to the moral law by adopting virtuous maxims of ends. This is to say that he fails to cultivate the deep motivating subjective ground of his maxims by reassessing his incentives in different situations. For this reason, the subjective principle of his particular maxims, or his disposition, remains impotent in practice.

## 5.4 Favourable Implications

My reading has promising implications. First, it opens up the possibility of accounting for the inner conflict experienced by the morally weak agent without making problematic assumptions about her possession of a good underlying maxim and her morally incorrect specific maxims. The weak-willed agent has the will to do what the moral law requires *in abstracto*, whereas *in concreto* she fails to make an effort to strengthen her will. Second, the proposed reading does not commit us to the view that the morally weak agent simply changes her mind by dropping her adopted principle. Third, it accommodates Kant's suggestion that moral weakness is expressed both at the level of adopting maxims and at the level of following them. The Kantian morally weak agent is also someone who lacks moral strength in constraining herself to adopt particular maxims that are powerful in practice. She wills the good but lacks a settled intention to determine her choice by diverting attention away from her inclinations and focusing on a particular moral end. She can be described not only as lacking an intention to perform an action in order to follow a maxim but also as lacking the intention that is essentially involved in adopting maxims of virtue. Fourth, by addressing the neglected connections between weakness, moral strength, moral feeling and the activity of setting ourselves moral ends, this reading highlights important aspects of moral weakness that have been overlooked thus far. Fifth, it enables us to distinguish the weak from the impure and the vicious. Finally, it does not compel us to abandon the incorporation thesis in order to save the phenomenon of weakness of will, and it can tell us why moral weakness counts as moral evil. In a certain way, the morally weak agent takes an active stance regarding her inclinations. However, she still fails to enter into a state of actual self-determination because her moral intention is not firm in the sense of continually engaging in the purifying (or self-controlling) activity that the free adoption of maxims of virtue requires.

## 6 Concluding Remarks

Our examination of the capacity for self-control as the ability to *abstract from* sensible impressions has found support in textual evidence and has challenged a merely instrumental reading of Kant's take on self-control. This has highlighted the sense in which self-control is central to Kantian virtue. When explained as abstraction at two levels, self-control can also be necessary for setting ourselves moral ends.

Applying this reading of self-control has allowed us to see Kant's conceptions of moral strength and moral weakness in a new light. In the absence of this application, we might be tempted to read these concepts in terms of whether or not one is able to compel oneself to perform an action that one judges to be morally necessary and has chosen independently of one's capacity for self-control. This move is unacceptable for several reasons, however. For one, it reduces Kant's notion of virtue to a kind of skill needed for following already-established maxims, which means that we must account for the fulfilment of duties of virtue in the same way that we account for the fulfilment of duties of right. By claiming that virtue as moral strength is simply about compelling ourselves to undertake certain actions in order to adhere to our established maxims, we lose a useful tool for explaining the essence of Kantian virtue.

In other words, we put ourselves in a position of being unable to explain how we compel ourselves to adopt virtuous maxims of ends. As explained in the previous chapter, there are also reasons why Kantian moral weakness cannot be understood as a mere failure to follow our otherwise morally good maxims.

Some scholars shy away from the claim that Kantian virtue is self-control at its essence. They likely want to avoid the caricature of the Kantian virtuous agent as excessively self-controlled and hostile to emotions and feelings. I think that we can counter this objection by providing a fuller account of Kantian moral self-control. My attempt to reconcile the different terms that Kant uses to describe this phenomenon has led to an acknowledgment of the essential role of moral feeling in self-determination and the adoption of virtuous maxims of ends. By paying closer attention to the cultivation of our capacity for feelings, I have shown that it makes sense to interpret Kant's notion of cultivation as the activity of acquiring the strength of self-control. This enables us to consistently claim that the cultivation of our moral feelings can in a certain sense be involved in the process of adopting maxims of virtue. This may be surprising, but reading self-control in terms of abstraction also leaves room for other feelings, such as our sympathetic feelings. In short, it makes it possible to retain the necessary, emotional component of Kantian virtue.[70]

One might still object that abstracting from sensible impressions, like every other type of 'stepping back' or reflectively disengaging, results in a merely theoretical, abstract stance, and that the agent who practices this regularly will eventually become completely divorced from every-day life.[71] This 'moral' agent will be incapable of moral action, because she will fail to set herself particular moral ends. In truth, however, it seems that the proposed interpretation of self-control takes us a good distance from such an agent. Since abstracting from certain sensible impressions involves redirecting our attention to something else, it enables us to focus our attention on particular moral ends.[72] Moreover, on my account, abstracting from certain feelings and desires need not be an activity of practical reason that is entirely external to feelings and desires. It seems that reflective distancing need not be conceived of as a completely unemotional distancing of reason.

My reading of self-control as abstraction also offers a plausible proposal for how to understand the relation between the empirical perspective and the pure

---

[70] Alix Cohen (2018) holds that focusing on discussions of virtue as strength of will leads us to neglect feelings. I hope to have shown that this is not the case.

[71] By accentuating the cognitive basis of virtue, Merritt (2018) ingeniously deals with this objection by putting forward a novel view of reflection. I take another route, which focuses more on self-control, ethical end-setting and the motivational aspect of virtue.

[72] This also reminds us that not only the form of our maxim, but also their content or ends are important.

## Kant on Self-Control

perspective in Kant's doctrine of virtue. According to this proposal, these perspectives are not only different but also intertwined.[73] It remains to be seen how this idea can be further developed, but for now we can note that the picture of abstraction presented above demystifies the meaning of the term 'pure' in Kant's doctrine of virtue. The Kantian agent reasoning about moral issues decides not to take into account certain sensible representations, without being able to banish them from her mind. In line with this, Kant describes the human being, understood as *homo noumenon*, as 'a being endowed with *inner freedom*' (MM 6: 418) [italic in the original].

Our analysis of how self-control and moral feeling, as subjective conditions, relate to the idea of purity, allows us to appreciate the full relevance of Kant's moral psychology within his own moral theory. These psychological conditions are not only means to observing maxims of virtue but also their necessary conditions.

Clarifying the distinct character of Kant's conception of moral self-control also gives us the opportunity to apply his conception to contemporary issues in moral psychology. Analysing self-control as the Kantian ability to redirect attention and set ourselves moral ends sheds new light on the ongoing dispute over how self-control and weakness of will are to be understood. Although Kant, unlike Aristotle, understands virtue as self-control, existing approaches are usually Aristotelian and an empirically supported Kantian approach to self-control has yet to be developed.

---

[73] My aim was not to explain human action merely from an empirical perspective, as Patrick Frierson tries to do (2005, 2014).

# References

## 1 Primary Sources

References are to Kants gesammelte Schriften. Ausgabe der Preussischen (later Deutschen) Akademie der Wissenschaften (Berlin: Georg Reimer, subsequently Walter de Gruyter, 1900). Except where indicated otherwise, translations are based on the Cambridge Edition of the Works of Immanuel Kant, eds. Paul Guyer and Allen Wood (Cambridge: Cambridge University Press, 1992).

References to Kant's works are given using the following abbreviation scheme:

| | |
|---|---|
| Anth | *Anthropology from a Pragmatic Point of View* |
| CF | *Conflict of the Faculties* |
| CJ | *Critique of the Power of Judgement* |
| CPR | *Critique of Pure Reason* |
| CPrR | *Critique of Practical Reason* |
| G | *Groundwork of the Metaphysics of Morals* |
| ID | *Inaugural Dissertation* |
| L-Anth | *Lectures on Anthropology* |
| L-Eth | *Lectures on Ethics* |
| L-Met | *Lectures on Metaphysics* |
| MM | *The Metaphysics of Morals* |
| NMM | *Kant's Notes to the Metaphysics of Morals* |
| PM | *What Real Progress Has Metaphysics Made in Germany Since the Time of Leibniz and Wolff?* |
| Rel | *Religion within the Boundaries of Mere Reason* |
| TP | *On the Common Saying: That May be Correct in Theory, but it is of No Use in Practice* |

## 2 Secondary Sources

Allison, Henry E. (1990). *Kant's Theory of Freedom*. Cambridge: Cambridge University Press.

Allison, Henry E. (1996). *Idealism and Freedom: Essays on Kant's Theoretical and Practical Philosophy*. Cambridge: Cambridge University Press.

Bagnoli, Carla (2003). Respect and Loving Attention. *Canadian Journal of Philosophy*, 33, 483–515.

Baron, Marcia W. (1993). Freedom, Frailty and Impurity. *Inquiry*, 36, 431–41.

## References

Baron, Marcia W. (1995). *Kantian Ethics Almost without Apology*. Ithaca: Cornell University Press.

Baxley, Anne Margaret (2003). Autocracy and Autonomy. *Kant-Studien*, 94, 1–23.

Baxley, Anne Margaret (2010). *Kant's Theory of Virtue: The Value of Autocracy*. Cambridge: Cambridge University Press.

Baxley, Anne Margaret (2015). Virtue, Self-Mastery and the Autocracy of Practical Reason. In Lara Denis and Oliver Sensen (eds.), *Kant's Lectures on Ethics: A Critical Guide*, Cambridge: Cambridge University Press, pp. 223–39.

Borges, Maria (2019). *Emotion, Reason and Action in Kant*. London: Bloomsbury Academic.

Cagle, Randy (2005). Becoming a Virtuous Agent: Kant and the Cultivation of Feelings and Emotions. *Kant-Studien*, 96, 452–67.

Cohen, Alix (2018). Kant on Moral Feelings, Moral Desires and the Cultivation of Virtue. In Dina Emundts and Sally Sedgwick (eds.), *13/2015 Begehren / Desire*, Berlin: De Gruyter, pp. 3–18.

Davidson, Donald (1980) [1969]. How Is Weakness of the Will Possible? In Donald Davidson (ed.), *Essays on Actions and Events*, Oxford: Clarendon Press, pp. 21–42.

Denis, Lara (2006). Kant's Conception of Virtue. In Paul Guyer (ed.), *The Cambridge Companion to Kant and Modern Philosophy*, Cambridge: Cambridge University Press, pp. 505–37.

De Witt, Janelle (2018). Feeling and Inclination: Rationalizing the Animal within. In Kelly Sorensen and Diane Williamson (eds.), *Kant and the Faculty of Feeling*, Cambridge: Cambridge University Press, pp. 67–88.

Engstrom, Stephen (1988). Conditioned Autonomy. *Philosophy and Phenomenological Research*, 48, 435–53.

Engstrom, Stephen (2002). The Inner Freedom of Virtue. In Mark Timmons (ed.), *Kant's Metaphysics of Morals: Interpretative Essays*, Oxford: Oxford University Press, pp. 289–315.

Fahmy, Melissa Seymour (2009). Active Sympathetic Participation: Reconsidering Kant's Duty of Sympathy. *Kantian Review*, 14, 31–52.

Frierson, Patrick R. (2005). Kant's Empirical Account of Human Action. *Philosophers' Imprint*, 5, 1–34.

Frierson, Patrick R. (2014). *Kant's Empirical Psychology*. Cambridge: Cambridge University Press.

Goy, Ina (2013). Virtue and Sensibility. In Andreas Trampota, Oliver Sensen and Jens Timmerman (eds.), *Kant's 'Tugendlehre'*, Berlin: De Gruyter, pp. 183–207.

Grenberg, Jeanine (2010). What Is the Enemy of Virtue? In Lara Denis (ed.), *Kant's Metaphysics of Morals: A Critical Guide*, Cambridge: Cambridge University Press, pp. 152–70.

# References

Gressis, Rob (2010). Recent Work on Kantian Maxims I: Established Approaches. *Philosophy Compass*, 5, 216–27.

Gressis, Rob (2010). Recent Work on Kantian Maxims II. *Philosophy Compass*, 5, 228–39.

Guyer, Paul (2000). *Kant on Freedom, Law and Happiness*. Cambridge: Cambridge University Press.

Guyer, Paul (2005). *Kant's System of Nature and Freedom: Selected Essays*, Oxford: Clarendon Press.

Guyer, Paul (2010). Moral Feelings in the Metaphysics of Morals. In Lara Denis (ed.), *Kant's Metaphysics of Morals: A Critical Guide*, Cambridge: Cambridge University Press, pp. 130–52.

Henden, Edmund (2008). What Is Self-Control? *Philosophical Psychology*, 21, 69–90.

Hill, Thomas E., Jr. (2002). *Human Welfare and Moral Worth: Kantian Perspectives*. Oxford: Clarendon Press.

Hill, Thomas E., Jr. (2012). *Virtue, Rules and Justice: Kantian Aspirations*. Oxford: Oxford University Press.

Johnson, Robert (1998). Weakness Incorporated. *History of Philosophy Quarterly*, 15, 349–67.

Johnson, Robert and Cureton, Adam (2017). Kant's Moral Philosophy. In Edward N. Zalta (ed.), *The Stanford Encyclopedia of Philosophy* (Spring ed.), https://plato.stanford.edu/archives/spr2017/entries/kant-moral/.

Kahn, Samuel (2015). Kant's Theory of Conscience. In Pablo Muchnik and Oliver Thorndike (eds.), *Rethinking Kant*, Vol. 4, Cambridge: Cambridge Scholars, pp. 135–56.

Karbowski Thomason, Krista (2017). A Good Enough Heart: Kant and the Cultivation of Emotions. *Kantian Review*, 22, 441–62.

Kennett, Jeanette (2003). *Agency and Responsibility: A Common-Sense Moral Psychology*. New York: Oxford University Press.

Kleingeld, Pauline (2017). Contradiction and Kant's Formula of Universal Law. *Kant-Studien*, 108, 89–115.

Korsgaard, Christine M. (1989). Kant's Analysis of Obligation: The Argument of Foundations I. *The Monist*, 72, 311–40.

Louden, Robert (2011). *Kant's Human Being: Essays on His Theory of Human Nature*. Oxford: Oxford University Press.

McCarty, Richard (1993). Kantian Moral Motivation and the Feeling of Respect. *Journal of the History of Philosophy*, 31, 421–35.

McCarty, Richard (2009). *Kant's Theory of Action*. Oxford: Oxford University Press.

## References

Mele, Alfred (1987). *Irrationality: An Essay on Akrasia, Self-Deception and Self-Control*. Oxford: Oxford University Press.

Merritt, Melissa (2018). *Kant on Reflection and Virtue*. Cambridge: Cambridge University Press.

Mischel, Walter (2014). *The Marshmallow Test: Mastering Self-Control*. New York: Little, Brown.

Nyholm, Sven (2017). Do We Always Act on Maxims? *Kantian Review*, 22, 233–55.

O'Neill, Onora (1989). *Constructions of Reason: Explorations of Kant's Practical Philosophy*. Cambridge: Cambridge University Press.

Papish, Laura (2007). The Cultivation of Sensibility in Kant's Moral Philosophy. *Kantian Review*, 12, 128–46.

Papish, Laura (2018). *Kant on Evil, Self-Deception, and Moral Reform*. New York: Oxford University Press.

Peters, Julia (2018). Kant's Gesinnung. *Journal of the History of Philosophy*, 56, 497–518.

Schönecker, Dieter (2013). Kant's Moral Intuitionism: The Fact of Reason and Moral Predispositions. *Kant Studies Online*, 1, 1–38.

Sherman, Nancy (1990). The Place of Emotions in Kantian Morality. In Owen Flanagan and Amélie Oksenberg Rorty (eds.), *Identity, Character and Morality*, Cambridge, MA: The MIT Press, pp. 149–70.

Sussman, David (2001). *The Idea of Humanity: Anthropology and Anthroponomy in Kant's Ethics*. New York: Routledge.

Timmermann, Jens (2000). Kant's Puzzling Ethics of Maxims. *The Harvard Review of Philosophy*, 8, 39–52.

Timmermann, Jens (2006). Kant on Conscience, 'Indirect' Duty, and Moral Error. *International Philosophical Quarterly*, 46, 293–308.

Timmermann, Jens (2022). *Kant's Will at the Crossroads: An Essay on the Failings of Practical Rationality*. Oxford: Oxford University Press.

Timmons, Mark (1994). Evil and Imputation in Kant's Ethics. *Jahrbuch für Recht und Ethik*, 2, 113–41.

Vujošević, Marijana (2014). The Judge in the Mirror: Kant on Conscience. *Kantian Review*, 19, 449–74.

Vujošević, Marijana (2017). *The Subjective Conditions of Human Morality: The Relevance of Kant's Moral Psychology*. Groningen: University of Groningen.

Vujošević, Marijana (2019). Kant's Account of Moral Weakness. *European Journal of Philosophy*, 27, 40–55.

Vujošević, Marijana (2020a). Kant's Conception of Moral Strength. *Canadian Journal of Philosophy*, 50, 539–53.

Vujošević, Marijana (2020b). The Kantian Capacity for Moral Self-Control: Abstraction at Two Levels. *Archiv für Geschichte der Philosophie*, 102, 102–30.

Ware, Owen (2009). The Duty of Self-Knowledge. *Philosophy and Phenomenological Research*, 79, 671–98.

Ware, Owen (2014). Kant on Moral Sensibility and Moral Motivation. *Journal of the History of Philosophy*, 52, 727–46.

Watson, Gary (1977). Skepticism about Weakness of Will. *The Philosophical Review*, 86, 316–39.

Watzl, Sebastian (2022). Self-Control, Attention, and How to Live without Special Motivational Powers. In M. Brent and Lisa Miracchi (eds.), *Mental Action and the Conscious Mind*, New York: Routledge, pp. 272–300.

Wehofsits, Anna (2020). Passions: Kant's Psychology of Self-Deception. *Inquiry: An Interdisciplinary Journal of Philosophy*, 66, 1184–208.

Wilson, Eric Entrican (2015). Self-Legislation and Self-Command in Kant's Ethics. *Pacific Philosophical Quarterly*, 96, 256–78.

Wood, Allen W. (1999). *Kant's Ethical Thought*. Cambridge: Cambridge University Press.

Wood, Allen W. (2008). *Kantian Ethics*. Cambridge: Cambridge University Press.

Wood, Allen W. (2018). Feeling and Desire in the Human Animal. In Kelly Sorensen and Diane Williamson (eds.), *Kant and the Faculty of Feeling*, Cambridge: Cambridge University Press, pp. 88–107.

Wood, Allen W. (2020). *Kant and Religion*. Cambridge: Cambridge University Press.

Cambridge Elements

# The Philosophy of Immanuel Kant

### Desmond Hogan
*Princeton University*

Desmond Hogan joined the philosophy department at Princeton in 2004. His interests include Kant, Leibniz and German rationalism, early modern philosophy, and questions about causation and freedom. Recent work includes 'Kant on the Foreknowledge of Contingent Truths', *Res Philosophica* 91 (1) (2014); 'Kant's Theory of Divine and Secondary Causation', in Brandon Look (ed.) *Leibniz and Kant*, Oxford University Press (2021); 'Kant and the Character of Mathematical Inference', in Carl Posy and Ofra Rechter (eds.) *Kant's Philosophy of Mathematics Vol. I*, Cambridge University Press (2020).

### Howard Williams
*University of Cardiff*

Howard Williams was appointed Honorary Distinguished Professor at the Department of Politics and International Relations, University of Cardiff in 2014. He is also Emeritus Professor in Political Theory at the Department of International Politics, Aberystwyth University, a member of the Coleg Cymraeg Cenedlaethol (Welsh-language national college) and a Fellow of the Learned Society of Wales. He is the author of *Marx* (1980); *Kant's Political Philosophy* (1983); *Concepts of Ideology* (1988); *Hegel, Heraclitus and Marx's Dialectic* (1989); *International Relations in Political Theory* (1992); *International Relations and the Limits of Political Theory* (1996); *Kant's Critique of Hobbes: Sovereignty and Cosmopolitanism* (2003); *Kant and the End of War* (2012) and is currently editor of the journal Kantian Review. He is writing a book on the Kantian legacy in political philosophy for a new series edited by Paul Guyer.

### Allen Wood
*Indiana University*

Allen Wood is Ward W. and Priscilla B. Woods Professor Emeritus at Stanford University. He was a John S. Guggenheim Fellow at the Free University in Berlin, a National Endowment for the Humanities Fellow at the University of Bonn and Isaiah Berlin Visiting Professor at the University of Oxford. He is on the editorial board of eight philosophy journals, five book series and The Stanford Encyclopedia of Philosophy. Along with Paul Guyer, Professor Wood is co-editor of The Cambridge Edition of the Works of Immanuel Kant and translator of the Critique of Pure Reason. He is the author or editor of a number of other works, mainly on Kant, Hegel and Karl Marx. His most recently published books are *Fichte's Ethical Thought*, Oxford University Press (2016) and *Kant and Religion*, Cambridge University Press (2020). Wood is a member of the American Academy of Arts and Sciences.

### About the Series

This Cambridge Elements series provides an extensive overview of Kant's philosophy and its impact upon philosophy and philosophers. Distinguished Kant specialists provide an up-to-date summary of the results of current research in their fields and give their own take on what they believe are the most significant debates influencing research, drawing original conclusions.

# Cambridge Elements ☰

## The Philosophy of Immanuel Kant

### Elements in the Series

*Kant and Global Distributive Justice*
Sylvie Loriaux

*Anthropology from a Kantian Point of View*
Robert B. Louden

*Introducing Kant's Critique of Pure Reason*
Paul Guyer and Allen Wood

*Kant's Theory of Conscience*
Samuel Kahn

*Rationalizing (*Vernünfteln)
Martin Sticker

*Kant and the French Revolution*
Reidar Maliks

*The Kantian Federation*
Luigi Caranti

*The Politics of Beauty: A Study of Kant's Critique of Taste*
Susan Meld Shell

*Kant's Theory of Labour*
Jordan Pascoe

*Kant's Late Philosophy of Nature: The Opus postumum*
Stephen Howard

*Kant on Freedom*
Owen Ware

*Kant on Self-Control*
Marijana Vujošević

A full series listing is available at: www.cambridge.org/EPIK

Milton Keynes UK
Ingram Content Group UK Ltd.
UKHW020841130824
446880UK00009B/60